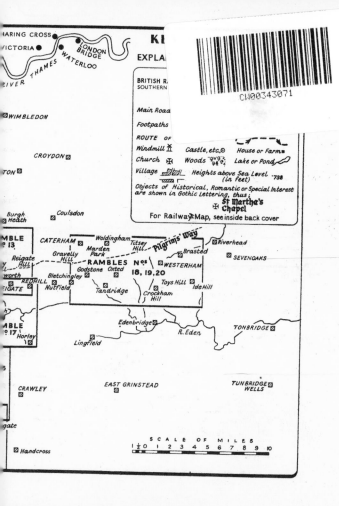

CHARING CROSS

VICTORIA   LONDON BRIDGE

WATERLOO

RIVER THAMES

KE[Y]

EXPLA[NATION]

WIMBLEDON

CROYDON

TON

BRITISH RA[ILWAYS]
SOUTHERN

Main Road ....
Footpaths ....
ROUTE OF ....
Windmill 🏚   Castle, etc. ⊙   House or Farm ■
Church ✠   Woods   Lake or Pond
Village   Heights above Sea Level ·738
(in feet)
Objects of Historical, Romantic or Special Interest
are shown in Gothic Lettering, thus :
✠ St Martha's Chapel

For Railway Map, see inside back cover

Burgh   Coulsdon
Heath

RAMBLE   CATERHAM   Woldingham Titsey   Riverhead
No. 13.   Gravelly   Marden   Hill   Pilgrims' Way
Reigate   Hill   Park   Brasted   SEVENOAKS
Hill   RAMBLES Nos   WESTERHAM
worth   REDHILL   Bletchingley Godstone Oxted   18, 19, 20
REIGATE   Nutfield   Tandridge   Toys Hill   Ide Hill
Crockham
Hill

RAMBLE   Edenbridge   TONBRIDGE
No 17   Horley   R. Eden
Lingfield

CRAWLEY   EAST GRINSTEAD   TUNBRIDGE
WELLS

gate

Handcross

SCALE OF MILES
1 ½ 0 1 2 3 4 5 6 7 8 9 10

SOUTHERN RAMBLES

FOR LONDONERS

By
S. P. B. MAIS, M.A.

SOUTHERN
BRITISH RAILWAYS
REGION

LONDON, 1948

CONTENTS

MAPS, ETC.

THE HANDY ELECTRIC TRAIN: FREQUENT SERVICES AT REGULAR
INTERVALS TO "RAMBLELAND" STATIONS OF SURREY AND SUSSEX

(*Above shows a London—Redhill—Brighton train*)

PREFACE

A S I said when I originally set out, "the object of this book is quite simple." It is to help you to indulge a very natural instinct, to obey a natural law. We are, like it or not, children of the earth, and to quote Professor G. M. Trevelyan, "removed from her our spirit withers or runs to various forms of insanity." We just have to get back to the country whence we were originally sprung or wilt away both in spirit and body. "Unless we can refresh ourselves at least by intermittent contact with nature we grow awry."

My object was (and is) to show you how most easily to get back and where you are most likely to find quietude and loveliness. The face of England has lately undergone and is still undergoing a very rapid change.

The War has left its sears on the countryside no less than on the towns. Once familiar landmarks have disappeared and, what is far worse from the walker's point of view, footpaths have been obliterated by the farmers and vast sections of common land seized by the War Department and churned into impassable morasses by tanks and other engines of war.

This is not the place to discuss whether these are the unavoidable penalties of progress and civilisation. My job is done when I pass on certain warnings. In this modern version of the "Pilgrim's Progress" I merely put up sign-posts. "Here is the Slough of Despond. Keep out" or "Here is Doubting Meadow. Here lie giants. Beware."

The old "Southern Rambles" would have been completely out-of-date even if there had been no war, for the simple reason that London's middle-aged spread is increasing. It is no use lamenting the fact that St. Mary Cray and Foot's Cray were lovely country villages when I was a boy. The fact has to be faced that they are no longer country villages.

You must realise that if you want real country walks you must accept the fact that the North Downs are now roughly London's outer bastion.

There are plenty of unexpectedly rich walks inside the bastion, but you never know when you walk out of a wood that you won't find yourself faced with a new satellite town or housing estate, so for the sort of walk I have in mind you ought not to leave the train till you get as far west as Guildford or as far south as Dorking, Redhill or Sevenoaks.

It so happens that the train services to the ideal starting-points are fast and frequent, so you won't have to spend more time in the train than you would have in going half the distance in the old days.

What has surprised me (and I am supposed to know my England) is the wealth of country that still remains unexplored within twenty-five miles of Charing Cross and Victoria.

The farmers may not have redeemed their promises to

reopen the public footpaths and bridle-tracks that they were allowed to plough up during the War. The War Department have certainly aroused the resentment of all country lovers for their high-handed action in earmarking the best walking country for their training areas—(Ockley Common and Chobham Ridges have to be seen to be believed)—but on the credit side no praise could be too high for the foresight of the Surrey County Council in preserving and signposting tens of thousands of acres of woodland, downland and commons in the Dorking area where you may wander at will and most certainly as easily get lost as if you were in the Northern Highlands or in the wilds of Central Wales.

Indeed so rich and profitable is the Dorking area that I have spent the greater part of a year in that one corner of Surrey tracing new (to me) tracks, each one lovelier and more sequestered than the one before.

I have changed my tactics. I am becoming more selective and learning wisdom. When I originally set out I fell into the trap of imagining the success of a walk to depend on its distance.

As an undergraduate I was never satisfied unless I covered about 35 miles a day. On my original Southern Rambles I set myself what politicians so oddly call "a target" of fifteen to twenty miles. It is only now that I have learned that a maximum of enjoyment can be got out of a walk of from eight to twelve miles. This allows of loitering to listen to birds singing, watching birds fly, picking and eating hazel-nuts, chestnuts, whortleberries, wild strawberries, blackberries, and so on, according to the season of the year, lying on thyme-scented downs and just gazing up into the blue or watching the clouds scurry by.

Best of all this allows of a margin of time in which to be genial in the bars of tiny village inns, to listen to the philosophy of a road-mender or shepherd and the problems of the farmer who is as ready to welcome the rambler who takes a knowledgeable interest in his beasts or crops as he is to set the dog on the ill-mannered or thoughtless stranger who breaks down his hedges or leaves his field gates open for the sheep to stray.

It is most important to remember that even if you fought against Germany to keep your England free, the right cultivation of the land lies in the hands of the farmers to whom you have entrusted it. You have no more right to trespass over his fields at random than you have to ride a horse over your neighbour's lawn or a bicycle up and down his garden path.

There are vast sections of Surrey and Kent that to our eternal advantage have been acquired for us and presented to us by the National Trust, a body that we owe it to ourselves and our children to support.

All over these counties you will find unobtrusive notices, the sign of the oak leaf, to denote the fact that you are now on your own land and have an owner's right to walk where you will. To select almost at random, Hindhead, Witley Common, Hydon's Ball, Albury Heath, Leith Hill, Hackhurst Downs, Bookham Common, Box Hill, Colley Hill, Crockham Hill, Toy's Hill, Ide Hill,

Finchampstead Ridges, Selborne Hill, South Hawke . . . all these and hundreds more places of exceptional loveliness are earmarked and preserved for your enjoyment in perpetuity. It is, of course, all too little, only a hundred thousand acres to set against the million acres seized by the War Department, and thirty-three million acres cultivated by the farmer. But it is something to be thankful for as you stand on one of these many Southern heights with all the wealth of the dim blue goodness of the weald stretching away below you towards the sea. It is something to know that this at any rate is not to be built over or (we hope) annexed as a military training area.

In my original tour I was so anxious to cover a large territory that I didn't mind a few miles of road walking.

The roads have become even more dangerous for the footslogger, and they have certainly become more unpleasant. My object this time has been to avoid roads altogether.

I have, of course, not always been successful in this, but you will find very little road-walking on any of these routes, as you will see by glancing at the maps.

The best plan, if the walk proper begins a mile or two outside Dorking, Guildford or any other town, is to take a bus as far as a stile or lane-end, and set your face resolutely against any road walking at all. Trudging along a road only ruffles the spirit instead of soothing it.

I am your guide to enchantment, not to discomfort.

Eschew therefore any walk which entails more than a hundred yards of high road. On the other hand when you find an obvious bridle-path so thickly entangled and overgrown through eight years' neglect and disuse you have an alternative choice, either to do what the farm-labourer has done and take the line of least resistance, which is to walk along the field-edge parallel with the path, or to take a billhook and spend a day in your fellow-ramblers' interest pruning the branches and treading down the established track.

There has been an attempt on the part of a few landowners to seize public bridle-paths and turn them into private drives. You have a perfect right to follow a public bridle-path even if it appears to be suddenly converted into a private drive. But you still have to keep to the path.

As usual on these travels I have always tried to elicit from local residents their ideas of the most worth-while walks. More often than not these enquiries have been fruitless. The average man appears to hop on a bus or train or get on his bicycle when he goes out unless he is on his way to cultivate his allotment.

I have found hotel managers, innkeepers and barmen singularly ill-informed about the footpaths in their area.

But I had one piece of astonishingly good luck. The booking-office clerk at Dorking Town station, Mr. Kenneth Taylor, revealed to me at least twenty walks in that area that I should certainly never have found for myself, and it is to him far more than to me that you owe thanks for opening up fresh vistas that you doubtless know as little about as I did before I met him.

The moral of this is go on enquiring even if ninety-nine out of every hundred of your enquiries lead you nowhere. I have had to walk in all weathers during this last year. I need scarcely point out that the most profitable month is the most colourful—June. Indeed, the same walk taken in June and in December will seem so different as to make you think it is a different one. But December has its compensations. If there is an absence of scent and colour there is a much wider view.

I have been turned back by snowdrifts but seldom by flood. The mud in the spring is deep enough to necessitate the wearing of heavy boots. Wet feet are unpleasant any way and the cause of many diseases. In these days of short commons you will be wise as far as possible to carry your rations with you. Hotels seldom cater for tea parties. On the other hand there are excellent cafés, notably in Godalming, Guildford and Dorking, where they provide home-made cakes.

As I live in Oxford I have had to spend many nights on these journeys away from home. I have usually found the Trust Houses reliable and inexpensive, but I must put in a special word for the White Horse at Dorking, which is not only good to look at but good to stay in. I found the food appetising, plentiful and agreeably varied. The walker no less than the angler appreciates good cooking and an assortment of poultry and game. At the White Horse I have known a choice of wild-duck, pheasant, pigeon, rabbit and chicken on the same menu.

I have tried out a new interlocking system on this tour.

By this means you can switch over from one walk to another, making it twice as long or half as long as the one I originally took. By means of a few permutations and combinations you have therefore the outline not of a mere twenty or so but of three hundred or three thousand walks all within an hour or so of London and all in country where you will hear no noise except that of a squirrel with nuts or a woodpecker pecking the bark of a tree, and see no living thing other than a scurrying rabbit or a whirring pheasant.

My object is not only to prove to you that there is good walking country in Surrey and Kent but that the cream of south country walking is to be found in those counties. I have therefore eliminated a number of quite pleasing walks in order to concentrate on walks that approximate to perfection.

Your object is to achieve as complete a change as possible from your ordinary life in office or street, to let your eyes roam at one moment over wide horizons with an unbroken vista of blue sky overhead and at another moment to concentrate on the myriad colours interwoven in the carpet under your feet. Your object is to regain your lost senses, the sense of hearing that has been dulled by traffic and by bombs, the sense of sight that has been obscured by poring over ledgers, the sense of smell which has been vitiated by living too much indoors.

The grand thing about walking is that you are never too young to start once you can stand upon your feet, nor too old to go on walking so long as you can stand on your feet.

It is the healthiest and cheapest exercise and the purest of human pleasures. Few things have added so much to the sum of human happiness as walking. You and I only really become ourselves out of doors. Moods of depression, sullenness and despair all drop from us as we take to the open road. There is a healing power in nature which is yet to be believed by those who have never tried that cure for our human ills. "I have two doctors" said Sir George Trevelyan, "My left leg and my right." So set out on foot.

But it does matter these days where you walk. So let me show you where.

PUBLISHERS' NOTE

While great care has been taken in the preparation of this book, the publishers are unable to accept responsibility for any loss or prejudice arising through any mis-statements or inaccuracies contained therein.

Further, the mention of any road, footway or bridleway in any part of the text or maps contained in this book must not be construed as indicating the existence of a public right of way.

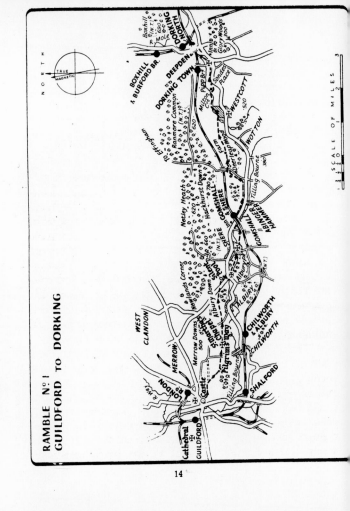

RAMBLE Nº I
GUILDFORD TO DORKING

NORTH

TRUE
MAGNETIC

SCALE OF MILES

RAMBLE 1

Guildford, St. Martha's Chapel, the Silent Pool, Shere, Gomshall, Dorking

IN the original edition of this book I did this walk the other way round and took a slightly different route.

I believe my latter route to be the more profitable.

In the first place it gives you more time to explore Guildford which is an ancient city of very great interest. To begin with there is the most imposing and graceful modern brick Cathedral which is in the process of construction on one of the spurs of the Hog's Back, a little removed from and overlooking the town. When it is finished it will be one of the outstanding ecclesiastical buildings of our time.

The main points of interest, however, lie in or just a little off the steep thousand-year-old High Street. These include the Lion Hotel where John Peel's hunting horn can still be seen, the eighteenth-century Cathedral Church of the Holy Trinity, which contains many ancient monuments, the sixteenth-century Grammar School, the Guildhall with a prominent clock that catches the eye all the way up the street, and most fascinating of all, the brick hospital of

[*Photo: Donovan E. H. Box*

CASTLE ARCH, GUILDFORD

Archbishop Abbot, founded in the early seventeenth century for the housing of ten old men and ten old women, crowned by tall brick turrets, Dutch gables, quaint-shaped chimney stacks and weather vanes.

The sequestered grass quadrangle is of great beauty, with old oak doors engraved like shells, a guest room with remarkable carvings, and hanging outside on the quadrangle wall is a shining brass bell for late-comers at night.

The Guildhall should certainly be visited for the sake of the very rich civic treasures, notably its fifteenth-century silver mace, and sixteenth-century ewer and basin. The oldest church in Guildford, St. Mary's, lies off the High Street. It has a Saxon tower, fine Norman arches and a gallery, but only a fragment of its once famous frescoes. The castle gateway still stands and also the ruins of the square Norman Keep built on a tree-fringed knoll. On the hillside above the castle stands The Chestnuts, the house in which Lewis Carroll died in 1898.

When your exploration of this exceptionally interesting old-world market town is over you will probably find yourself in agreement with William Cobbett, who said of it, "I think it is the prettiest and most agreeable and happy looking I ever saw in my life. Here are hill and dale in endless variety.

"Here are the chalk and the sand, vying with each other in making beautiful scenes. Here is a navigable river (the Wey) and fine meadows. Here are woods and downs. Here is something of everything but flat marshes and their skeleton-making agues."

Our journey begins almost opposite the great clock in the High Street where we turn through Tunsgate and keeping left walk up South Hill where we begin our climb up the middle road which is called Pewley Hill. Passing a house with the unusual name of "Just Here" we emerge after about ten minutes on to the open chalk downland where we immediately get a superb view of these hills and dales which won Cobbett's admiration. After keeping along the ridge for about two hundred yards you will see a fork, with a track descending right-handed into the hollow. The last time I took this walk I kept along the top of the ridge to Newlands Corner, but I think it is far more worth while to diverge here, and take this downward track because it leads to the famous church of St. Martha, the tower of which you can see crowning the tree-covered hill in the distance.

The track is narrow and overgrown but quite clearly defined. It passes by the side of an immense cornfield which they were cutting as I passed for I took this walk in the month of August.

At the foot of the hollow you leave the chalk and enter a sandy lane which is unmistakenly the ancient Pilgrims' Way. This soons leads to a road with some farm buildings and a large house nestling under the hill. You can either cross the road and continue along the track or turn right-handed up the road for a few yards as I did and then climb through a wicket-gate on the left above the farm which leads on to a knoll covered with heather and bracken and tall Scotch firs.

[*Photo : Donovan E. H. Box*

VIEW FROM PEWLEY HILL OF ST. MARTHA'S HILL

Bear left-handed, leaving the handsome thatched house on your right and you will then see the sandy track making its way under a wide avenue of trees, including one ancient oak of immense size, straight up the wood to the crest of the hill.

At the top of the hill, but not visible until you are clear of the trees, stands the solid tower and church of St. Martha, from the churchyard of which you can see seven counties.

Away to the west rise the wooded heights of

Blackdown and Hindhead. South you can see Leith Hill and the Weald of Sussex.

Immediately below you can pick out the river meandering among the parklands in the Albury valley. You can scarcely fail to be surprised and delighted by the wildness, variety and extent of the scene and exhilarated by the air which seems to sweep straight off the sea on to this high ridge which stands 600 feet above the sea. Inside the church I found a most informative verger who cycles up to this lovely spot every day of the year.

The church which a hundred years ago was a ruin, has been simply and neatly restored and looks well used. It has been slightly damaged by bombs.

After showing me a modern wooden carving of the saint the verger took me out into the churchyard to give me very precise instructions how to reach the Silent Pool.

There are a great many tracks leading down from the church so you have to pick your way carefully.

Facing due east take the wide sandy track as far as the concrete guard-post and then be careful to veer off to the left along a grass track which soon reaches the road. On the other side of the road take the gate that leads across a field, leaving the black roofed sheds on your left. You then come to a track which runs along the edge of a wood with nut trees all the way. At the bottom of the wood turn left along a lane for a hundred yards and then right when you come to some brick cottages where you follow a lane which runs along the bottom parallel with the Downs to the North. Within a few hundred yards you come to

ST. MARTHA'S CHAPEL

another lane. Turn right-handed down this lane about two hundred yards until you come to another row of cottages, and turn in left below them along a very narrow overgrown track which soon broadens out into a lane. This leads directly into a brickyard where I found it convenient to have my picnic lunch, after as varied a morning's ramble as one could desire.

The brickyard emerges on to a main road, where you turn right-handed for a hundred yards and then turn in left by a lodge to the famous Silent Pool. This is a small lake fringed with beech trees, the water of which is crystal clear and of a bluish colour with light green weeds at the bottom.

King John is supposed to have surprised a lovely peasant girl bathing here and to have driven her to drown herself to escape his unwelcome attentions. This is the only place I have ever seen tadpoles as late as August. This pool is well stocked with surprisingly large fish. Just beyond the pool the road joins the main Dorking-Guildford road.

Turn right (not left as you would expect) for a few yards and then turn up the track that runs just east of Albury's Catholic Apostolic church, which was built at a cost of £16,000 in imitation of the fifteenth-century style, by Henry Drummond, the banker.

The track leads into the lovely wooded park of Albury where you turn at once left-handed along a path which leads into a wood above the big house. The track through the wood bears right-handed and leads through a kissing-gate directly into a cornfield where there is a well-defined footpath. This brings you to a narrow "twitten" with a high wall on the right and then into a lane where you turn right to cross the tiny Tillingbourne and turn left past some cottages to the enchanting village of Shere. A line of weeping willows overhangs the river and the shingled spire of the ancient church calls you past the timber and brick houses that surround it to admire the richly carved chalk Norman porch and outside entrance to the west gallery, a very rare feature.

There are good glass and tracery in the windows and some attractive horse-box pews. There have been rectors of Shere since 1270.

Just opposite the south door take the narrow track

[*Photo: Donovan E. H. Box*

SHERE CHURCH

23

Here you turn right past a row of Council houses and then take a track on the left which leads directly on to the bank of the Pipp Brook again which you follow until you come to the main gates of Henley's and between those gates and the lodge stands Milton Court Lane.

Follow this lane and it will bring you out just by the old Pound at Sondes Place on to the main road just at the outskirts of Dorking with the tall and graceful church spire dedicated to the memory of Bishop Wilberforce straight in front of you.

As you wander along its wide main street you cannot fail to be impressed by the beauty of the famous old coaching inn, the White Horse, and you may even have time to search for the other famous inn immortalised by Dickens under the name of the Markis of Granby where Sam Weller met his mother-in-law.

The beauty of this walk lies in its variety. Within a distance of fourteen or fifteen miles you walk over chalk downs, along sandy tracks edged with bracken and heather, over fields, through woods, past about a dozen little ponds hidden in the trees, with glimpses of great houses standing in spacious parks, through farmyards and along the banks of a delectable meandering stream. There is no walking along main roads and your chances of meeting many other wayfarers are remote.

The Pilgrims' Way still miraculously preserves its quiet atmosphere in spite of the proximity of London.

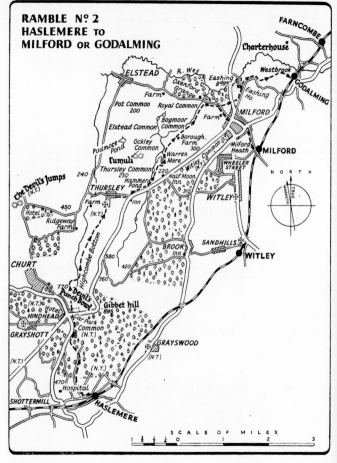

RAMBLE Nº 2
HASLEMERE TO
MILFORD OR GODALMING

FARNCOMBE

Charterhouse

Westbrook

GODALMING

ELSTEAD

R. Wey

Eashing Bdge.

Oxenford Grange

Eashing Ho.

Farm

MILFORD

Pot Common 200

Royal Common

Elstead Common

Bogmoor Common

Farm

Pudmore Pond

Ockley Common

Borough Farm

Milford Heath

MILFORD

Tumuli

Warren Mere

300

Witley Common (N.T.)

WHEELER STREET

240

Thursley Common 250

220

Half Moon Inn

NORTH

The Devil's Jumps (N.T.)

Hammer Pond

310

WITLEY

450

Hotel

Ridgeway Farm

Inn

Farm (N.T.)

TRUE MAGNETIC

BROOK Inn

SANDHILLS

WITLEY

Highcombe Bottom

580

420

CHURT

770

Devil's Punch Bowl

760

Gibbet hill 895

(N.T.)

Hotel

HINDHEAD

Car Park

GRAYSHOTT

Common (N.T.)

GRAYSWOOD (N.T.)

(N.T.)

(N.T.)

470

Hospital

SHOTTERMILL

HASLEMERE

SCALE OF MILES

¼ ½ 0 1 2 3

RAMBLE 2

Haslemere, Hindhead, Thursley, Ockley Common, Milford or Godalming

THE immediate and most natural objective of most walkers who leave the train at Haslemere is to make a bee-line for the heights to the north of Hindhead, but in spite of modernisation it is worth while first having a look round at some of Haslemere's remaining picturesque seventeenth-century houses with their warm-looking weather-tiled gables and tall brick chimneys.

There is a wide choice of ways to the top of Hindhead Common. Perhaps the most profitable route is to take the road at the north side of the railway line towards Shotter-mill and take the second turning to the right along it, turning left at the fork. After about a mile a track goes off to the left crossing the main Midhurst-Hindhead road and you then get a superb view westwards over Woolmer Forest and the hanging woods of Selborne.

Nearly two thousand acres of Hindhead Common and the immediate surroundings have been acquired by the National Trust, so you can wander at will on this famous upland more or less where you like. Most walkers make for Gibbet Hill which stands 895 feet above sea-level and provides about as wild and vast a panorama as you will

In Memory of
A generous but unfortunate Sailor
Who was barbarously murdered on Hindhead,
On Sep, 24, 1786.
By three Villains.
After he had liberally treated them,
And promised them his farther Assistance,
On the Road to Portsmouth.

When pitying Eyes to see my Grave shall come,
And with a generous Tear bedew my Tomb;
Here shall they read my melancholy Fate,
With Murder and Barbarity complete.
In perfect Health, and in the flow of Age,
I fell a Victim to three Ruffians Rage;
On bended Knees I mercy strove t'obtain,
Their Thirst of Blood made all Intreaties vain.
No dear Relation, or still dearer Friend,
Weeps my hard Lot, or miserable End;
Yet o'er my Grave a Stranger's Tears will flow,
For Portland, near Nottingham, was my Home.

[Photo: Donovan E. H. Box

THE SAILOR'S GRAVE, HINDHEAD

find in Southern England. The outstanding feature is less the distance you can see than the character of the scenery, though the distant views include the length of the South Downs and the Hampshire Downs. It is the only place in England that makes me feel that I am in Scotland.

Mile upon mile there is nothing to see but slopes covered with heather and bracken, knolls surmounted by pines, and dense woodlands. It seems quite absurd to think that London is almost visible.

Here there is real grandeur and (except at week-ends) complete isolation. The place is remembered by most visitors as the scene of a particularly sordid murder when nearly two hundred years ago an unknown sailor was set upon by three penniless men whom he had befriended on the road, and murdered. They were caught trying to sell the dead man's clothes and hanged in chains on the highest point in Hindhead. The only remarkable thing about this story is that it should still be remembered.

It is as well not to be in a hurry to leave the heights of Hindhead, for a fresh vista of delight comes into view with every knoll you climb, but when you decide to leave the uplands the best starting point is just to the east of the Huts opposite Thor's Hill Hotel.

There is a large flat parking place for cars on the Common here and at the far end of it a track descending steeply which almost immediately joins a wide sandy lane going left-handed under the hill. This is the route I took. As you can no longer see any landmark as soon as you reach this lane you have to guess your direction, but at the bottom of the hill a very deep lane goes off to the right which I took. This crosses the gully by way of a small stream at Highcombe Bottom and as I climbed up the southern bank I found myself on a wide track on a heather-covered common with a pine-covered knoll rising in front of me. I was now clear of the trees and followed the clearly defined track round the left side of the knoll, where I got fine views of the Devil's Punch Bowl as I looked back and to the north, of the Devil's Jumps to the north-west and in the far distance I caught a glimpse of the trees on Crooksbury Hill.

DIRECTION INDICATOR, DEVIL'S PUNCH BOWL

The track winds right-handed round the summit of the knoll and it is at this point that I left it to take a much older stony lane that led under the trees left-handed. If you keep along the broader track it will only take you on to the main road. This stony lane is long

GIBBET HILL

and straight and obviously very ancient, but it provides occasional glimpses of the stream running parallel in the valley to the left so that you have a guarantee that you are going in the right direction.

Eventually it leads to a farmhouse on the right, opposite which is a signpost which reads (pointing in the direction from which I had come) "Sandy track only to Punchbowl and Hindhead." It gives no indication that Thursley lies straight ahead. Apparently walkers are expected all to be moving in the same direction, southwards.

The lane, however, widens and a few more farms come into view, though the trees on either side form an

31

almost complete umbrella for a considerable distance. It was as I was walking along this lane that I met the only other ramblers that I encountered during the whole of that day. The lane now begins to twist and turn and eventually leads to the timber tower and steeple of Thursley church. It stands on a little knoll, with a very attractive square red-brick Georgian house just outside the churchyard. Instead of a clock it has a blue sundial in the tower and there is an exceptionally tall chestnut tree growing just inside the churchyard. Here are buried the sailor who was murdered at Hindhead two hundred years ago and in our time the poet John Freeman whose epitaph reads "John Freeman—poet. He was one of the poets who died too young, not yet quite fifty." There is a Saxon oven in the chancel, a plain square opening in the wall where the wafers were baked and the charcoal heated for the incense. But the most remarkable feature about the interior of the church is the collection of vast oak beams that rise up from four wooden piers in the middle of the nave to support the tower. The bell ropes hang through holes in these vast beams right in the centre of the church. The fact that they still use oil lamps in the church gives one a sense of the remoteness of the place. Just beyond the church there is a cluster of exceptionally attractive small timbered and tiled houses with unenclosed gardens bordering both sides of the road.

The lane comes out at a cross-roads exactly opposite the village post office. It was here that I made a fatal mistake. It is always a good thing on a walk to ask advice

INTERIOR OF THURSLEY CHURCH

B

33

whenever possible. My object was to cross Thursley Common, Ockley Common and Royal Common and then rejoin the train either at Milford or Godalming. The track was clearly enough defined on the map, and in the original edition of "Southern Rambles" I did this walk the other way on. I then said that I was pleased at the line I took because of the infinite choice of tracks. On this occasion the postmaster warned me that there were no tracks left at all as the tanks had churned up the whole area. He advised me to follow the main road until I came to the first Hammer Pond and then walk up by the side of the meres using them to give me my sense of direction. In view of what happened to me that is what I advise you to do.

If, however, you like complete wildness and a risk of getting lost do what I did. Immediately outside the Thursley post office there is a sandy track leading out on to the Common, if you can call this sand-swept waste a common. There were no tracks at all. I began by keeping my eye on the distant towers of Charterhouse but soon lost sight of them. I left a strange rectangular field that seemed very much out of place on my left, and after crossing a miniature Sahara climbed to a knoll with one tree standing on it and below saw an enclosed mound which was surrounded by barbed wire and marked "Ancient Monument. Out of Bounds." It was the only thing the tanks had spared. According to my map the track over Ockley Common to Royal Common runs just to the left of the place marked "Tumuli" so I veered off left to try and pick it up.

[Photo: Donovan E. H. Box
THE MOAT (NEAR ELSTEAD—THURSLEY ROAD)

Almost immediately I found myself off the sand-swept Sahara and in a land of impassable bog. If I had kept to the right of the tumuli I might have reached the line of the meres dry-shod. In my anxiety to get back on to dry ground I went so far to the left that very soon I found myself at the Moat, a mere that runs close to the road running up to Elstead. As I wanted to avoid road walking as far as possible I walked up this road only until I found another turning into the right which I was assured was a direct footpath to Royal Common. It certainly was a dry

OLD MILL, MILFORD

path and an attractive track through woodland but instead of bringing me out on to Royal Common it veered off far too much to the right and eventually to my very great surprise brought me out on the Portsmouth Road close to the Half Moon inn and the Polish Army Camp. It had carried me south-west instead of north-west. That taught me never to try to cross trackless country that has been over-run by tanks. For at least a couple of hours I had been completely lost in the heart of the Surrey Woods, with only the sun (to which I paid little attention) to give me a sense of direction. I am telling you all this by way of warning. If you wish to test your sense of direction try to find your way over Thursley, Ockley and Royal Commons. But if you want to avoid encounters with peat bogs and not to be lost for hours in wild woods keep along the road from Thursley till you come to the Hammer Pond and then work your way north by way of the meres and Borough Farm to Bagmoor Common and the lane that joins the Elstead-Milford road at Oxenford Grange. You can then take the road straight down to Milford station which is what I did, or (which I think is more interesting) make, by the less-frequented route, for Godalming.

This entails continuing along the track when the road turns sharply right-handed towards Milford. This track crosses the main road and joins the road that skirts Eashing House. After making a half-circle round the park you again leave the road by a track that takes you by way of Westbrook direct to Godalming station.

This walk is between twelve and fourteen miles long.

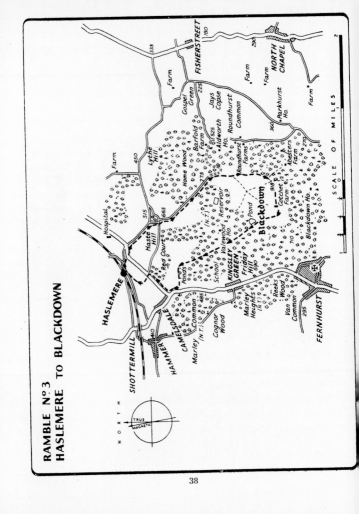

RAMBLE Nº 3
HASLEMERE TO BLACKDOWN

RAMBLE 3

Haslemere, Haste Hill, Blackdown

THIS is one of the wildest walks in the South of England, short but extraordinarily varied and beautiful.

It unfortunately necessitates a comparatively tedious walk along a high road though it is quite unfrequented in the middle of the week.

I kept south-east from Haslemere station to Haste Hill, and then came a long trek along a high-banked road with very prosperous-looking and attractive houses on both sides. Occasionally there are peeps between the thick trees which show above forests of bracken. The National Trust luckily possesses all this area, so pheasants rose from under our feet and flew unperturbed over our heads. The track eventually becomes sandy and winds over the bracken-covered common for what seems to be miles. The view is tantalisingly hidden until you get to the southern spur of Blackdown, where the reward is great, for the view extends over the Sussex weald to the whole range of the South Downs, south of Portsmouth and Pulborough. The chalk pits at Cocking stand up clear and bright and the whole range is visible from Butser to Chanctonbury.

The whole upland is so wild that it is difficult to remember that we are within an hour's train journey of

[Photo: Donovan E. H. Box

LOOKING OVER THE SUSSEX WEALD FROM BLACKDOWN

London. You can't lose your way, for there is only the one track running south-east the whole way from Haslemere.

This is one of those walks where it repays to go back the way you came, for having attained the heights of the Blackdown plateau, it is against the grain to go down into the valley after only a mile or two on the tops. I do not like too soon to leave the upland breeze blowing over the bracken and in any event the viewpoint seems quite different when you face northward and there are always unexpected glimpses of distant vistas seen through the trees. But if you prefer to make a circular tour of it there is a track on the south-western edge which descends steeply by way of Cotchet Farm after which you turn sharply right-handed along a path past some water which leads to the main road where you take the right-hand fork to bring you back to Haslemere station. Either way the distance is inconsiderable, not more than six miles, but you may well spend a whole day over it because whether you descend into the weald or wander back along the ridge, you will be wise to spend several hours on the crest, for I can think of no view south of the Scottish Highlands at once so extensive and so quickly changing with the time of day. To miss Blackdown is to miss one of the wonders of the South.

The great thing is not to allow yourself to be put off this walk because it requires few directions and entails for once walking along a straight road. The road is pleasant and the view when you reach it breath-taking in its beauty and quite bewildering in its variety.

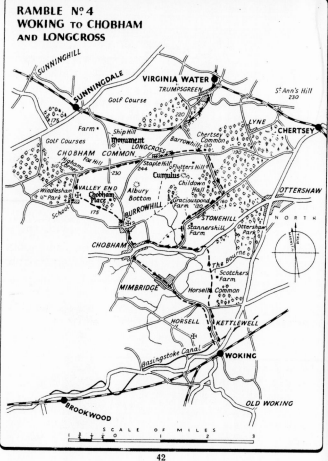

RAMBLE Nº 4
WOKING to CHOBHAM
and LONGCROSS

SUNNINGHILL

SUNNINGDALE

VIRGINIA WATER

TRUMPSGREEN

St Ann's Hill
230

Golf Course

220

LYNE

CHERTSEY

Farm

Ship Hill

Chertsey
Common

Monument

LONGCROSS

Barrowhills
130

190

Golf Courses

Fox Hill

CHOBHAM COMMON

Highams
Corner

310

230

Staple Hill
244

Flutters Hill

Cumulus

Childown
Hall

OTTERSHAW

Windlesham
Park

VALLEY END

Chobham
Place

Albury
Bottom

Graciouspond
Farm 120

160

School

175

BURROWHILL

STONEHILL

Ottershaw
Park

NORTH

CHOBHAM

Stannershill
Farm

MIMBRIDGE

The Bourne

Scotchers
Farm

Horsell Common

HORSELL

KETTLEWELL

Basingstoke Canal

WOKING

OLD WOKING

BROOKWOOD

SCALE OF MILES
1 ½ ¼ 0 1 2 3

that lies between two lanes and as soon as you reach the top of the field turn left. This path soon emerges into a lane where you cannot fail to be struck by the beauty of a large barn with steep pitched roof nestling by a timber and brick manor house with medieval tall chimneys and many dormer windows. You turn first left and then right past this house and find yourself on a signposted road just opposite a very attractive house called Pilgrims. This road leads into the village of Gomshall where there is a good inn called the Black Horse. There are ponds and watercress beds all along the south side of the road and you soon pass the exquisite long, low brick and timber Hatch Farm with its hanging brass bell and a little further on come to Abinger Hammer with its remarkable clock that projects high over the roadway. It contains the figure of a smith, striking the hours with his hammer and bears the motto "By me you know how fast to go." There is still a smithy and a carpenter's shop, and the carpenter told me that there are tracks all across the park of Abinger Hall. I didn't try any of them but continued about half-a-mile along the high path running above the road until I came to the road marked Effingham. Turn left up this road through the avenue that leads to Deerleap Wood. At the far end of this wood there is an open gate and well-marked track on the right which skirts the wood and leads past the buildings of Park Farm. The track here is broad and well-defined and leads through woods and over fields to the cottages of Westcott where you turn left-handed to cross the Pipp Brook at Baldwin's Lane.

RAMBLE 4

Woking, Horsell Common, Chobham, Valley End, Higham, Foxhill, Staple Hill, Longcross, Chilldown, Stonehill, Woking

WOKING is an admirable centre for walking. Not only is the surrounding country full of variety, but it has the advantage of an excellent frequent and fast train service to Waterloo.

There are two Wokings. Old Woking stands a mile or so to the south of the station, on the banks of the Wey, and is relatively quiet and sequestered. It has had a long and honourable history. Originally it was a royal residence of William the Conqueror.

There are still traces of the royal palace at Woking Park Farm where Henry VIII, Edward VI, and Elizabeth often stayed. In the end it was granted by James I to Sir Edward Zouch, a member of the Royal Household, in exchange for £100 in gold and fish for dinner on St. James's Day. There is a memorial to Sir Edward Zouch in the old church which is partly Norman and partly Jacobean.

New Woking on the north side of the station is a very large thriving residential town which owes its size and quick evolution to the railway. When the station was built in 1838 it stood alone with an inn on an otherwise

43

deserted heath. It contains one of the only two Mohammedan mosques in the country.

I set out northward on leaving Woking station through Kettlewell to Horsell which has a fourteenth-century church containing several interesting brasses. I left the road here to strike across Horsell Common by a track that leaves Scotcher's Farm a little on the right, and after crossing the Bourne emerges on the Chertsey road a little to the east of Philpot Lane.

Here I turned left along the wide margined quiet lane that leads to Chobham village which has miraculously preserved an atmosphere of complete unsophisticated old-world charm in spite of its close proximity to towns and military camps.

It is a village of singularly varied and beautiful houses, some of them cigar-box shaped and built of Queen Anne brick, some timbered, some yellow-washed. The shops are real village shops, with low ceilings and age-old polished counters where customers stay to gossip as they do in the very cosy old-world picturesque White Hart inn. The church is of white stone, built by the Normans, with a very low steep-pitched roof and a stout tower surmounted by a shingle spire. There is a remarkable font with its eight sides panelled in oak and a fine ancient chest.

After exploring this most attractive and oddly unexploited village, I turned northward leaving Burrowhill on my right and just beyond a triangular green I took the lane on my left which skirted the grounds of Chobham Place, and found myself in a world of bracken and silver birches with several extremely attractive black and white houses, all of them thatched, peeping out from the woods. This lane led me to Valley End where there is a school and a new brick church. Just beyond here I turned right-handed up a wooded lane with a very large estate on my left hand, once the home of the Shelleys and recently taken over as a convent. This brought me out at Higham Corner where an inviting track between the trees leads straight on northwards to Kingshill and the Sunningdale golf course. I resisted the temptation to take this path because I wanted to explore the wilderness of Chobham Common, and a wilderness it has certainly become, for just after I turned right-handed leaving two strange-looking knolls on my left that had been badly cut up by military vehicles, I came to Fox Hill which is now covered by a vast array of army huts, the first section of which I found occupied by German prisoners of war and the second by squatters.

I was now on the summit of the wild open common with fifteen gaunt pines standing on the summit of Staple Hill, from which I had a glorious view southward of the whole ridge of the Hog's Back and Merrow Downs beyond the tall chimney that is Woking's outstanding landmark, and northward of the dense woods of Windsor Forest.

But, alas, the tracks across the common had all been obliterated by the tanks which had churned up the once lovely heather-covered moorland and left a water-logged morass of potholes and concrete blocks.

In the summer it is a sand-swept desert, and in the winter an impassable bog.

[*Photo : Donovan E. H. Box*

STAPLE HILL, CHOBHAM COMMON

46

To cross this trackless no-man's land might be good training for commando fighting, but it is not my idea of a pleasant peace-time ramble, so instead of making for Albury Bottom as I did when I last crossed Chobham Common, I kept along the firm high road where there was no danger of sinking in the bog, and the view continued to be extensive.

Away on my left stood the monument that marks the spot where Queen Victoria reviewed her troops in 1853, and I could not help wondering what she would have thought of the tank that was even at that moment lumbering and lurching about like a primeval mastodon over the churned-up common just outside the enormous tank factory that has been established below the crest of Staple Hill.

Immediately in front of the factory I saw the first tank ever to have been invented standing like George Stephenson's "Rocket" as a proud pioneer, the forerunner of a mighty race of new destructive giants.

The curious thing is that within a mile I passed quite suddenly into a land where there was no trace of tank activity. The whole of the common had been transformed into an undulating sea of mud and deep water-logged craters, but on the further side of the common the fields were green and the woods rose high on both sides.

Behind a belt of tall trees I saw the fine estate of Barrow Hills, the country-seat of Lord Camrose, and at Chertsey Common I turned right-handed round Flutters Hill where the woods were being cut and passed a poultry farm bearing the attractive name of Echoing Green, after which the way was lined with magnificent silver birches.

And so I came to the bracken-covered woods of Chilldown where the fences were all down and a myriad tracks led to the sites of war-time ammunition dumps, now of course cleared away. I turned right-handed at the foot of the hill still skirting the Chilldown woods till I came to Stonehill where the broad sandy track from Gracious Pond Farm came in. This is the track that I took last time when I was able to cross the common by way of Albury Bottom. From this end it looked innocent enough, but I shuddered to think where I should have been stuck had I been fool-hardy enough to leave the firm going and follow in the wake of the tracks over the ruined common.

At Stanners Hill there were inviting tracks going off into the bracken on both sides of the way, and I passed some attractive small houses peeping out between the trees and the gorse. Just beyond Stanners Hill Farm there is a track going off to the right which takes you back to Chobham either by way of Burrowhill or by the lane that passes Chobham Park Farm, but I kept on left-handed past Larkinshaw, a fine brick house with a gazebo rising above one corner of its high walls. This way soon brought me back on to the main road and the warm hospitality of the White Hart at Chobham where I enjoyed an excellent meal before returning to Woking by way of Mimbridge and Cox Hill Green. This walk is about seventeen miles in length or rather more, but it can easily be shortened by taking a bus back to Woking from Chobham.

[Photo: Donovan E. H. Box

WHITE HART INN, CHOBHAM

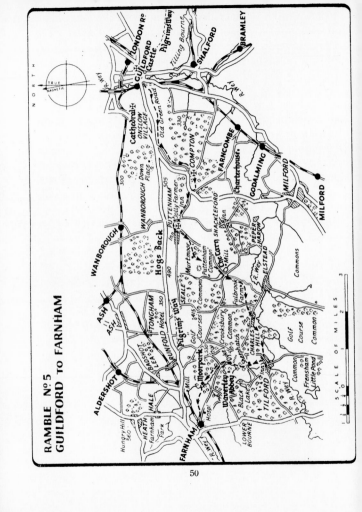

RAMBLE No. 5
GUILDFORD to FARNHAM

RAMBLE 5

From Guildford, by way of Compton, Puttenham, The Tarn, Charles Hill, Tilford, Waverley Abbey and Moor Park to Farnham

I REGARD this as perhaps the most rewarding of all Surrey walks. I owe the idea of it to the manager of the Lion Hotel, Guildford, who is an enthusiastic discoverer of unknown byways in the county.

Almost as soon as you leave Guildford station you find yourself on the main Portsmouth Road, as heavily congested as any road in this island.

But at the foot of the High Street you will be surprised to find that its continuation westwards, so far from carrying a great body of motor traffic, carries no traffic at all.

This is known as the old Green Road, and it was up this very steep deserted old road that I climbed out of Guildford westwards.

It is so steep that it reminded me of the hill at Clovelly, and indeed one of the houses perched precariously above its precipitous green bank is aptly called Clovelly.

It is a metalled road with houses for a few hundred yards, but on the top, which is the summit of the Hog's Back, it becomes a cinder track with a wide grass verge on either side bounded by high hedges.

51

WATTS MEMORIAL CHAPEL, COMPTON

There is a kissing-gate on the right which it is well worth going through in order to follow the green track on the outside of the hedge that runs parallel with the old road, for the views to the north over the new Cathedral extend over a tremendous stretch of heathland as far as the Chiltern Hills. Another kissing-gate at the end of this patch of downland, the slopes of which are thickly covered with stunted thorns, leads back into the old track. It is possible now to follow the way on the southern side of the hedge which provides a quite different vista of densely wooded hills to the south, including Hindhead, Black-down and Hydon's Ball.

After about two miles, the Portsmouth Road comes in on the right crossing over the Hog's Back diagonally, but just before it joins the continuation of the old Green Road there is another road falling steeply down to the left. This leads directly to the very attractive village of Compton where I revisited the famous shingle-spired church. On no account miss this church which is one of the most remark-able in the country. Here are some of the features to look out for. In the first place there is a sanctuary with Norman wooden rails above the altar, the only example in Britain, there are remains on one side of a Saxon anchorite's cell, and on the other, of a Norman anchorite's cell, with the ancient wood polished and rubbed where the anchorites placed their elbows, fingers and thumbs.

In the east window is the oldest piece of stained glass in the country. It is Norman and depicts the Madonna and Child. Close to the pulpit is a rough drawing done perhaps with a dagger, of a Norman knight accoutred for the crusades with a strange cross by his side with the cross of St. Andrew superimposed on it.

The nave, walls and tower of this very ancient church are Saxon and the chancel is Norman, as are the piscina in the upper sanctuary and the aumbry and piscina in the lower sanctuary. The capitals and plaster decorations are all very remarkable and bear no resemblance to any others that I have seen.

[Photo: Donovan E. H. Box

SHOWING OUTER ORNAMENTATION OF
WATTS CHAPEL, COMPTON

Lovers of the artist G. F. Watts will want to spend longer in the village to visit the terra-cotta and red-brick Watts Chapel and Art Gallery where hang about a hundred of his famous pictures, bequeathed by him to the nation and on view every day of the week except Thursday. Outside the Art Gallery is a collection of terra-cotta pottery.

Retracing my steps a little to the

54

north of Compton church, I found a lane going westwards at the end of which is a footpath which brought
me back on to the main road. Here I turned right-handed
for a few yards, and then turned left along the road that
runs on the south side of Puttenham Heath. Just past the
Jolly Farmer inn I again turned left and was soon in
Puttenham where men were at work mending the clock
face on the red and grey fifteenth-century church tower.
The pews have been well restored in modern oak and there
are four fine stout Norman arches.

Puttenham is a cosy village of red-brick and tiled
cottages. Just outside the Good Intent inn I met a man
painting some house railings who assured me that the field-
path was apt to get very wet and advised me to follow the
lane almost opposite the inn.

The alternative way (that I intended to follow) lies
half-way along the village and then veers left by a track
that leads on to Puttenham Common.

The route I took soon links up with this and is
certainly dry. I followed the lane south-west until I came
to a sandy track on the right, and this lead me past two
cottages, through a wood and emerged on the top of
Puttenham Common by a house called Murtmoor. I was
totally unprepared for the scene that here unfolded itself.
Up to now the landscape had been genial and quiet
cultivated land.

I now found myself overlooking a wild undulating
piece of open country, covered with bracken with occasional clumps of pines. There were wide tracks in every

direction. I took the one that struck out over the common south-west and this brought me out on to the road again, just before it crossed the Tarn.

At the Tarn I loitered on the bridge looking out on a wide still lake over which one heron was lazily flying and from the tree-fringed banks of which a solitary angler was lazily fishing. At the south end of the lake was a lofty very attractive mill. The whole scene was one of quite outstanding beauty and I was surprised to find that I had it almost to myself. It may, for all I know, be crowded at week-ends, but in mid-week it still remains completely unspoilt, the undisturbed haunt of singing birds and waterfowl. On the south side of the bridge there is a most attractive avenue of oaks running north-west and south-east.

I continued along the road which was now hedgeless with inviting tracks continually going off right and left under the silver birches.

There was a tremendous expanse of shrub and tree, and magpies and jays screeched and flew out above tangled overgrowth that was in places quite reminiscent of a jungle.

There I came to my first house, Fulbrook Farm on my right, a most attractive square house of flint with tarred barns with red-tiled roofs.

Just at the entrance to the farm stands an inconspicuous notice almost covered by foliage. It reads: "Elstead Parish Council. Bridle-Path to Tilford." This is one of the very few signposted bridle-paths that I encountered west of Guildford.

[*Photo : Donovan E. H. Box*

BANKS OF THE TARN NEAR PUTTENHAM

I turned in along this track which was well defined for a few yards. Then the bridle-path quite suddenly became a narrow impenetrable mass of undergrowth that quite effectively blocked the way between the two hedges.

Walkers and farm-workers had left the bridle-path to die and made a new track along the edge of the field by its side. There has been so little walking on footpaths of recent years that there is grave danger of tens of thousands of public bridle-paths becoming irretrievably lost unless parish councils or walkers in large numbers open them up again.

It would certainly be to the farmer's advantage to see them opened up, because he least of all wants walkers to take to the field side of the hedge if there is a narrow defined path between hedges.

According to the map this track leads straight across a road and pursues its course in a straight line, but when I emerged on to the road I was faced with an open drive and the words "Three Barrows Place" on a board on either side.

As this looked like a private drive I went up and down the road for some distance to find a notice about the continuation of the bridle-path.

There was none, so I had no alternative but to enter the drive, where I saw the continuation of the bridle-path almost at once.

There were notices on either side, and quite legitimate notices, warning wayfarers that the woods to right and left were private, but there was no parish council or other notice to direct attention to the fact that the sandy bridle-path was public. This part of the walk was quite enchanting. I was treading on a soft green carpet of moss. There were heathery rides going off on both sides. It was firm and dry underfoot with a great variety of trees, from eating chestnut to beech towering above me.

This part of the walk, which cuts across a tiny slice of the south-east corner of Crooksbury Common, gave me a very strong desire to explore more of so rich a common, and the map shews three or four tracks that cut right across the heart of it. I only hope that these rights-of-way are being jealously preserved, because the whole of this section of the walk was outstanding in variety and beauty and seemed very little trodden.

This track emerges on to the road at Charles Hill where I found a most convenient inn, the Half Way House, a cosy picturesque house with a most hospitable hostess who greeted me with the astounding statement that she had more drinks than she could sell. As a native she deplored the passing of the footpaths and made one extremely apposite comment. "Decent people," she said, "who don't like to trespass go miles out of their way round the roads through fear of being on private ground."

On leaving the Half Way House I climbed the hill past one drive gate until I came to an unobtrusive turning exactly opposite Gate Cottage.

There is a beech tree guarding its entrance on the north and a sweet chestnut on the south. It ought, of course, to be signposted, but it isn't.

TILFORD BRIDGE [*Photo: Donovan E. H. Box*

It is an unmistakable public track and provides a
boundary between two properties. It passes first through
a kissing-gate to a pine wood, then crosses two drives to
a private house and later emerges on to a heather common
with a wire fence on either side. At the top of a particularly
wild gorge a stoat stood up and chattered indignantly as I
passed. At Highmead I crossed a road and I was surprised
at the number and magnificence of the large houses that
lay half-hidden in the thick woods. Then there came a
clearing and a wonderful view out over Frensham Heath
to Hindhead. After this the track suddenly emerged on to
a new made-up road and a succession of new and pleasant

60

houses. Keeping to the left at a fork, I was soon in Tilford, a most attractive village on the banks of the Wey, which is here spanned by two bridges, one, an ancient stone bridge with wooden railings. There is a large triangular village green on one side of which stands the famous King's Oak which William Cobbett described as "by far the finest tree I ever saw in my life." It is 26 feet wide. Tilford was the home of one of our best known early great cricketers, "Silver Billy" Beldham who lived to be 96. It was also the home in later years of Philip Snowdon.

There are many rivers in England where you may walk for miles along the river bank. The Wey is not one of them.

I turned right-handed just past the post-office along a track that ran alongside the winding water-meadows of the Wey for a little distance. At the first fork I kept left and along a sandy lane which led up to the crest of a hill where I passed the white house of Till Hill, entered a wood and kept as straight a line as I could, disregarding tracks veering off right and left. This brought me to the farm at Sheep-hatch where I crossed the road to the obvious continuation of the track to Waverley. The track was now a woodland ride that led round the foot of some very singular bracken-covered knolls marked on the map as prehistoric dykes.

I turned left on emerging on to the road and found myself facing Stella Cottage, a very attractive square flint-and-stone house with french windows.

I turned left to cross the bridge spanning the Wey and as I crossed it a kingfisher darted from under it.

On the left I found the gates to Waverley Abbey open but a most curious notice barred the way. It read "No admittance to Waverley Abbey Ruins until grass is cut."

In point of fact it is easy to see the ruins across the lake from this notice-board. They are certainly picturesque, standing as they do embowered among trees above the still waters of the lake, but not so picturesque as Tintern, of which we are reminded, because that too is a Cistercian foundation, but Waverley is older. Founded in 1128 it is the oldest Cistercian house in England.

I retraced my steps past Stella Cottage and turned in at the open gate next-door into a drive where a notice warns the public that access is denied to motorists and cyclists.

This wide sandy track passes first the sinister-looking watery cave where the witch Mother Ludlam once lived (her cauldron still remains in the tower of Frensham church), near the steep sandhills where Cobbett used to roll down as a child, and Jonathan Swift used to climb before breakfast. The Wey on the left has now become a wild swamp with stunted trees and shrubs, a paradise for duck and other wild fowl. The avenue itself is lined with lime trees, and sand-martins' nests can be seen in the bare sandy rocks that lead up to the woods, and at the end of the drive I came to the famous four-storeyed mansion of Moor Park, always, as I remember it hitherto, neat, its walls shining white, and gardens of great splendour.

The War has left it derelict and overgrown. This is a place of very poignant memories. It was here that Dorothy

[*Photo : Val Doone*

WAVERLEY ABBEY

Osborne and Sir William Temple after so many years of separation because they were on opposite sides in the Civil War, ultimately settled down to a long happily married life. It was here that Temple wrote his famous essay on Gardening, and it was here that his young secretary Jonathan Swift met the young Esther Johnson, who was destined to become his dearest companion and earn immortality as Swift's Stella. It was while he was at Moor Park that Swift wrote "The Tale of a Tub," the book that Cobbett regarded as one of the greatest in the world. Temple and Dorothy Osborne were both buried in Westminster Abbey, but Temple's heart was laid in a silver box under the sundial in his favourite garden. Perhaps it is still there.

I turned left at the modern ugly, red-brick gatehouse of Moor Park, crossed the Wey and then turning right-handed climbed a high-banked lane with pines growing on the tops of the banks and occasional fine views of the wide water-meadows below, and so by way of Old Compton Lane I came to the main road and Farnham station.

If you have time, however, before catching your homeward-bound train you should go on to see William Cobbett's birthplace, the Jolly Farmer inn, a most picturesque solid yellow house with a gabled end and a low-ceilinged bar which can scarcely have altered since Cobbett was alive. The church where Cobbett lies buried is also well worth a visit, for in spite of a rigorous restoration it is still noble. Most interesting of all there is the famous castle which became the Palace of the most eminent bishops of Winchester.

Its central earthwork, where the shell-keep stands, dates from pre-Conquest days. The great Norman Keep towering over the town was built by Henry of Blois. It was captured by the Dauphin of France when he was in pursuit of King John, and in the Civil War it was first held by a Commonwealth leader George Wither who was a poet and later taken by a Royalist poet, John Denham. When Wither was taken prisoner Denham pleaded that his enemy's life should be spared on the ground that so long as Wither was alive, he (Denham) would not be the worst poet in England.

One of the most famous bishops of Winchester who lived here was Bishop Morley who spent £11,000 on repairing the damage done to it in the Civil War. He lived in a cell, slept on a stone couch, ate only one meal a day, never had a fire, never married, was never ill, and lived till he was 87. He gave up one of his rooms to Isaak Walton who was at that time engaged on the writing of biographies of famous Divines.

Quite apart from its very considerable literary associations, its historic background and its famous castle, Farnham is worth exploring for the sake of its domestic architecture (it is especially rich in Tudor and eighteenth-century houses) and its general atmosphere which is not very easy to define, but contains a happy combination of dignity and modern congeniality. It is one of the few ancient great historic towns to have kept the best of its past. This walk is about twelve miles.

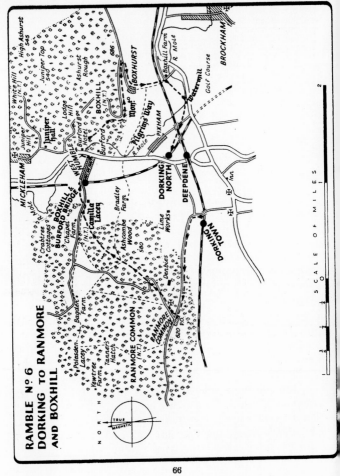

RAMBLE Nº 6
DORKING TO RANMORE
AND BOXHILL

SCALE OF MILES

RAMBLE 6

Dorking, Ranmore Common, Polesden Lacey, Camilla Lacey, Burford Bridge, Box Hill, Pilgrims' Way, Boxhurst, Watermill, Dorking

I BEGAN this walk by turning left-handed immediately after leaving the station yard of Dorking Town station, which is ideally placed for the walker, because it lies right at the foot of the Downs.

There is a footpath above and parallel to the road that runs past Denbies Park on the southern side, and from this path which is shaded by trees I got glimpses as I climbed up of the green valley below and the thick woods leading up to Leith Hill on the further slopes.

At the top of the hill, which is about 600 feet above sea-level, I came out on to Ranmore Common where the hedgeless road is bordered by a very wide green verge on both sides.

On the north side there are any number of equally inviting green tracks disappearing into the woods. You can with equal advantage take any one of three of these.

The first lies a few hundred yards to the west of the post office that stands at the road junction.

This takes you through the woods of Ranmore Common to Tanner's Hatch, where you veer right-handed skirting Polesden Lacey to take the lane to Bagden Farm.

Alternatively you can make a bee-line through the woods to Bagden Farm by turning east at the post office

[Photo: Donovan E. H. Box
POLESDEN LACEY HOUSE

and taking the broad track that enters the woods exactly opposite Ranmore church, the spire of which is a notable landmark for miles.

The track that I took on this occasion entered the woods about a hundred yards further east than the Bagden Farm track and this perhaps is the most richly rewarding of the three, though they are all quite exceptionally attractive.

The track was wide and mossy, and almost immediately crossed a road on the further side of which seven posts had been erected, presumably to prevent motorists from exploring the depths of the forest in their cars. The way now became sandy with seas of burnished bracken on both sides with oak trees and holly bushes rising above the bracken. I saw plenty of horses' hoofmarks and indeed these woodland tracks are as ideal for riding as they are for walkers, but I met neither walker nor horseman the whole day.

I seemed to have strayed into a lost ancient world on this wooded plateau, for there was no sound but the screeching of jays, the whirring of disturbed pheasants and the almost noiseless scampering of grey squirrels among the branches of the firs above my head.

There were many paths going off to the left into the depths of the woods, but I kept straight on until I came to a broad clearing of close-cropped grass bordered with bracken where I got a magnificent view northward of the woods leading to Bagden Farm. At the end of this clearing there was a choice of three ways, stretching in front of me like three fingers. An old post that stood by the middle one may once have been a signpost. Certainly a signpost is badly needed in all these woods. After a little hesitation I chose the middle track which dived steeply down into a wild wood of yew trees and eating chestnuts. I had the feeling that I had stumbled on to an ancient way that may very well have been one of the many tracks that the pilgrims took on their way from Winchester to Canterbury. It was wide enough to take a coach and four and deeply sunken below the level of the rest of the wood. After curving gently right-handed for some distance it led me to the bottom edge of the wood where I saw for the first time since I started a vista of fields on my left and a distant view of a great mansion on the further hill in front.

My track now joined a lane that came in from the right and I walked under an avenue of beeches down the left-hand side of a large field of roots until I came to a track at the bottom of the field bearing right-handed. This track was signposted "Footpath only." Just to the left I saw the ruins of an ancient chapel in a farmyard, and at the end of the field where the footpath joins the road I was standing under the shadow of the famous tree under which Fanny Burney wrote, and looking with more than ordinary admiration at the charming two-storeyed, creeper-covered square house that is Burney Cottage. I had arrived at Camilla Lacey, surely one of the loveliest sounding of all English place-names.

Fanny Burney built her cottage at Camilla Lacey out of the profits she made from her novel "Camilla."

The old house was burnt down but it is worth turning up the lane for a few yards to see the high-walled gardens on the left and the fine stone porch of the house on the right which is bordered by an exceptionally tall yew hedge which I passed when I regained the road.

The Pilgrims' Way runs close by, but has been cut up

and enclosed by a new building estate called Pilgrims Close. These new houses are extremely attractive.

The lane comes out at the gatehouse of Leladene. I here crossed the railway bridge above Box Hill station and at the end of the road, which is called West Humble Street, I turned left over the bridge that spans the Mole to the famous and picturesque white Burford Bridge Hotel where Keats wrote "Endymion" and Nelson spent his last hours before sailing for Trafalgar and parted for the last time from Lady Hamilton.

Immediately beyond the hotel on the northern side is the broad and very steep chalk track that leads to the summit of Box Hill. A notice to the effect that "Bicycling is Prohibited" seemed unnecessary in view of the fact that it is quite difficult enough to walk up the first part of the steep bank which would make an ideal ski-ing slope but would scarcely permit of an acrobat to remain in the saddle of a bicycle. I suppose this walk up Box Hill is the most popular hill walk in the country if not in all the world, but on this sunny cold October day with the frost coating the chalk under the shrubs, I encountered no living soul the whole way up or down.

It is a walk to be taken at a very leisurely pace. In the first place it is worth diverging from the track left-handed to look down over the steep smooth green gully to Lodge Hill, Juniper Top and the slopes where George Meredith lived during his latter years. In the second place it is worth coming back again and again as you climb higher to the edge of the escarpment to look at the wealth of yew and box and juniper which cover the steep sides of the hill and also pick out the unexpected line of fine cypress trees that cast long shadows along the valley of the Mole.

I came out at the top of the hill at the Fort Tea Gardens, just beyond which is a clearing where I got one of the most magnificent views in the South of England. There is a semi-circular stone monument erected to the memory of Leopold Solomons who gave Box Hill to the Nation in 1914, and on this stone are arrowheads showing the direction of some of the more outstanding features of the landscape that are visible on a clear day.

These include the whole range of the North Downs to Reigate, Crowborough Beacon, East Grinstead, Mount Harry, Lewes, the Devil's Dyke, Shoreham Gap and Chanctonbury Ring on the Sussex Downs, and far away to the west I could discern the heights of Hindhead.

This is indeed a vast panorama. A road runs eastward along the top of the ridge, but there is plenty of room to walk along the wide grass verge with splendid views all the way.

After about a mile I came to an open-air swimming pool and thereafter the way lies between houses, so I then took the right-hand track that led steeply down to join the Pilgrims' Way at the foot of the hill. Here I turned once more right-handed along slopes dotted with juniper and yew until I came to Boxhurst where there is a narrow footpath on the left running between two fences which at the bottom end is signposted "Footpath." This led me to a lane which passed under a railway arch and exactly

VIEW FROM BOX HILL

73

CASTLE WATERMILL, DORKING

opposite where a road comes in at right-angles on the left I climbed the steps on to a field path. This led me over a weir of the Mole to a very ancient weather-boarded water-mill which still retains its old blackened wooden mill-wheel.

Just opposite the mill is a most curious cave hollowed out of the rock with ferns growing on its wet sides.

I turned right-handed past the mill along a footpath which leads direct to Dorking North station. As I wanted Dorking Town I left this after a few yards to take a short steep track on my left which brought me out on the Dorking road exactly at the new Watermill Restaurant and Swimming Pool.

Within a half an hour I was back in the town at the picturesque White Horse Hotel after a glorious switchback walk of some seven miles.

RAMBLE Nº 7
DORKING to LEITH HILL

RAMBLE 7

Dorking, The Rookery, Tillingbourne, Friday Street, Leith Hill, Coldharbour, Lower Merriden Farm, Redlands Wood, Dorking

THIS, mainly woodland, walk is generally acknowledged to be one of the finest in the South Country.

On the day I chose for this revised walk the colouring of the trees, varying from light amber to dark mahogany, was quite wonderful. The air was crisp and cold. The time was late October. A correspondent had suggested that, instead of starting at Wotton as I did on my previous walk over this area, I should be better advised to walk up Rose Hill, cross the Nower and then go on by way of Bury Hill and Westcott Heath. I was warned that the way was blocked up by Army huts at Bury, so I took a bus from Dorking for a threepenny fare as far as the Rookery, and I believe this to be the best starting-point of all.

I entered the wide lodge gates at the Rookery and entered a well-defined track which, at Rookery Cottage (a most picturesque little house), took the right-handed fork where there is a signpost marked "To Leith Hill." This led me over a stream, and I then skirted a lake on my left and took the narrow track that led through two wicket-gates steeply up between fences to the hill-top where the track disappears completely as the field across which it ran has been ploughed up, but by skirting the plough on the right-hand side of the field I came to a lane going left and right.

According to the map there is a track dipping down into the valley here, but a number of derelict Army huts now occupy it and a notice marked "Private" made me decide to turn left along the lane which runs pleasantly above the secluded valley, past a big house on the right.

This led me to Tillingbourne, which appears to consist of one half-hidden cottage on the left of the road and a most unexpected fountain of water in the very centre of the valley. Just before this fountain I crossed a stile on my right leading across the valley and the river by way of a well-defined, broad, raised green bank which enters the woods about halfway up the opposite hill. You need to exercise great care when you come to the gate at the entrance to the woods, for, instead of following the obvious path, you have to turn right-handed and after a few yards take the quite well-defined, narrow, very steep track that leads directly to the crest of the hill. Here I crossed a small, very attractive common which led to a stile, on the further side of which was a road which I crossed to continue the track. This led steeply downward for one field and I then turned sharp left along the middle of three tracks. Very soon I arrived at a large cosily-placed brick farm, nestling in a fold of the hills among the trees, and turned right-handed at the farm-gates to follow a clear broad, sandy track which was signposted "Footpath to Friday

WATERFALL, TILLINGBOURNE

BEECH WOODS, FRIDAY STREET

Street." In a minute or two I was peeping through a clearing at that most sequestered and lovely of all Surrey pools which lies in a deep hollow with great banks of bracken surmounted by tall pines on the further side and its edges fringed by a cluster of old brick cottages. There was no one visible and the only noise I heard was that of the water-fowl on the surface of the lake and somewhere a baby crying. I followed the lane round the right-hand side of the lake to the famous Stephan Langton inn, which has been rebuilt on a most lavish scale, but at the hour I passed (10.15) was quite deserted. It opens at 10.30. Almost all the cottages beyond the inn bear notices to the effect that they supply teas. I am not surprised Friday Street, in spite of its fame, remains unspoilt, a pure gem.

I passed one or two solitary walkers who were exercising their dogs along the narrow sandy lane which kept alongside a tiny trickling stream until I came to Abinger Bottom, where I encountered three elderly ladies at the junction of two forks who strongly advised me to keep straight on and join the road if I wished to avoid getting lost. As my whole object was to avoid roads I disregarded their advice and took the left-hand fork which bore up the hill a little way and then entered a farm gate on the right. This led me up a sandy lane past a field on my left which was full of caravans. At the top of the rise the track peters out, but, by skirting a field on the left edge, leaving a large house and two high aerial masts on my right, I came out on to a road just at the entrance to Foxholt. I turned right along this road, which is hedgeless and embowered with trees, until I came to a house on my right, opposite which I took a broad track with telegraph poles which plunged right through the heart of a quite thick wood.

This track soon joined a broad cinder track going off to the left, which I followed for some distance, until it veered off suddenly more to the left than I needed and so I deserted it to follow a narrow sandy track across which many trees had fallen in a gale.

I could see by the clearings on my right that I was by now near the edge of the escarpment, and the track brought me out exactly at the Monument at Leith Hill just an hour after leaving Friday Street. In view of the great height and massive proportions of this tall tower it is odd that you don't see it until you are within a few yards of it, but the woods are extremely thick all the way along and hide any sign of it. Leith Hill Tower was built by Richard Hull, of Bristol, who died here in 1772 and was buried under the foundations. The hill itself is 966 feet above sea-level at this point and those who scale the tower have the satisfaction of knowing that they are 1,000 feet above the sea. No other hill-top in the whole of the South rises as high as this. The views from it are quite magnificent. On this particular day I could see over the patchwork of vivid green fields and dark woodlands of the Surrey and Sussex Weald to the long pencil line of the South Downs, though I could not see the water of the English Channel through Shoreham Gap owing to the haze hanging over the Downs.

When I got to the tower I had the whole tremendous scene to myself, but before I had fully taken in the splendid

LEITH HILL TOWER

vista that lay unfolded before me I saw a troop of over a hundred schoolgirls come clambering up the steep sides. The mistress in charge told me that they had come to the foot of the hill by motor coach from Sayer Croft Camp at Ewhurst. One of the girls seemed to be much more excited by the splendour of the scene than the others, and her eyes were glowing with happiness as she turned and said to her companion, "Isn't it lovely to be in England?" It struck me as a most fitting but entirely unexpected comment from a schoolgirl.

A young man walking alone then appeared out of the woods and expressed great disappointment at finding the tower locked, and then a grey-haired lady coming from the opposite direction volunteered the information that the tower only just escaped being hit by a flying-bomb. The schoolgirls were meanwhile lining the edge of the hill and being instructed in the points of the compass, and the grey-haired lady warned me, if I wished to reach Coldharbour, not to go off to the right, as I should only come up against barbed wire and have to come back. Indeed, the way east from Leith Hill provides a bewilderingly wide choice of footpaths. It begins innocently enough by descending a steep gully, but on the further side there are at least six tracks. I kept to the middle one, which provided me with two unforgettable views, one to the north over a dense forest as far as the eye could see, and the other to the south of a large lake immediately at the foot of the very steep escarpment. There were yellowing leaves, silver birches, then a glade of old oaks, then a fox-

VIEW FROM LEITH HILL   [Photo: H. D. Keilor

glove in full flower (on 24th October), whortleberry
bushes just turning colour, and whole seas of bracken,
like burnished copper. And suddenly from a clearing I
got another tremendous view of all the shining chalk pits
and lime of the North Downs from Box Hill to Colley
Hill and Reigate.

The main point to remember with so many tracks to
choose from is to keep the high fence always on your
right. Do not be tempted to cross it.

There is a specially well-defined broad sandy track
just to the left of the fence which leads straight down to the

village of Coldharbour, and comes out exactly opposite the Plough inn. The landlord of this inn is not a walker. Very few landlords of inns are knowledgeable about footpaths. Yet it was upon his advice that I decided not to make for Holmwood, as I did the last time I did this walk, but try a zig-zag footpath route back to Dorking.

Exactly opposite the Plough inn is a broad lane signposted as "Public Footpath" that leads to Lower Merriden Farm.

Just before reaching the farm there is another sign "Public Footpath" leading off right-handed down into a gully. I disregarded this and went on to the farm where a woman was attending to numbers of minute poodles and pekinese who did their best to drown our voices, but she was so ecstatic about the virtues of the path I had disregarded that I retraced my steps to try it. She was right.

After crossing the foot of the gully, acting on her advice, I took a wide mossy woodland-drive bearing left which was just as picturesque as and rather similar to the Hobby Drive at Clovelly. It must be centuries old and is as wide as a carriage drive. It winds round the side of the hill and seems to go on for miles under an arch of silver birches and beech trees. It eventually brought me out on the road exactly at the gamekeeper's cottage at Robbing Gates. The path that I intended to take by way of Collickmoor Farm comes out on to the same road about a hundred yards further on.

I crossed the road at Robbing Gates to take a wide track that led past the palings of the reservoir into the heart of Redlands Wood which seems to consist mainly of eating chestnuts.

If you keep to the better marked right-handed track it brings you out on to the main road by North Holmwood church, but I was anxious to get back on to the less-frequented road, so I kept on taking the left-handed track whenever there was choice (and there were many) and this brought me down at the foot of the wood to a field-track going left-handed which soon brought me back on to the road about a mile to the south of Dorking. I kept along this deserted road for about eight hundred yards.

Just before I got to the Nower I passed at Ormesdale one of the most colourful gardens I have seen anywhere in Surrey.

Then I turned aside over a stile to climb the bracken-covered sides of the Nower in order to look over the town of Dorking to Ranmore Common and Box Hill on the one side and the magnificent lake below Bury Hill on the other. I there encountered the park-keeper and found my-self in entire agreement with him when he said "Whether you look into Dorking from here or out of Dorking from here there are few more agreeable sights in the whole South Country." "Agreeable" struck me as a most apt word for Dorking, but quite inadequate to express the glorious combination of rich woodlands and smooth downs that surround it. To reach Dorking I took the footpath at the northern foot of the Nower leading eastwards which brought me over fields into the town. This walk is about twelve miles long.

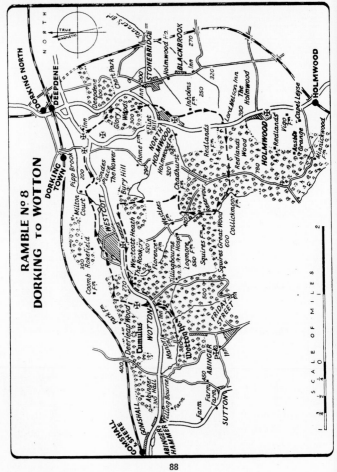

RAMBLE Nº 8
DORKING to WOTTON

Dorking, Glory Wood, Stonebridge, North Holmwood, Holmwood Common, the Lord Nelson, Redlands Wood, Chadhurst Farm, Westcott, Wotton

IN the middle of Dorking High Street on the south side there is a narrow archway where there is an inscription "To Glory Wood." It is a straight track and very easy to find and Glory Wood is indeed glorious, for it is. a fine and ancient wood, with fine and extensive views over Ranmore. I followed the track due south across the bypass to the new building estate at Stonebridge. Here I crossed the brook and turning left past the brickworks soon found myself at North Holmwood where I visited the uninteresting church and then took the track just outside the church which going due south brought me out on to a wild common of gorse and bracken. I followed this and I came to a green with an inn—the Lord Nelson, where I found a track going directly up through Redlands Wood where I got a glorious view of Colley Hill and the chalk pits on the sides of the North Downs. The woodland rides were thick with bluebells growing in great profusion on both sides. A singularly sweet smell permeated the whole wood. There were tracks going off in all directions but I took the one that led me straight up to the top of the

A "PEEP THROUGH" FROM GLORY WOODS

hill where I found myself in a misty sea of bluebells and whortleberry bushes below silver birches and tall pines. Although it was only afternoon nightingales were chanting in the bright May sunshine. I passed the railings of a reservoir on my right and saw many trees felled in a clearing. I turned left along a sandy track and soon came to a road. I crossed this road and turned a few yards to the right where I took an inviting track on the left that led me steeply down through a wood of tall oaks with more and more bluebells. On the left I noticed a path marked "Private" and continued on my way down to the valley where I came to a road where I turned right for about five yards and then took a narrow track that led me over a tiny clear amber-coloured stream to a ride with more and taller oaks and bluebells and marsh marigolds carpeting the right-hand slopes. Then the ride became a mossy way with rhododendrons growing on either side.

The stream ran all the way by my right side and I came to a field of roots which led me to a sandy track. This crossed the brook and almost at once joined a road running right and left. On the further side stood a stile over which I climbed as it was signposted "Public Footpath." This led me over a field with a wood on my left. Just over the crest of the hill I came to Chadhurst Farm on the further side of which I found a lane running left-handed. I followed this to a field on the left-hand side of which I found a plainly marked field-path which led me directly to the lake in front of the big house at Bury Hill.

After passing through a kissing-gate I came to a model

hamlet of brick houses with lattice windows and turning left I walked up to the Wotton Hatch Hotel in the hope of getting tea. To my surprise I found it locked, bolted and barred against me, so I crossed the road to take the sandy track that led to Wotton church, a very noble stone building standing on a knoll with bracken, broom, and gorse growing on its sides.

The interior of the church is uninteresting except for the Evelyn chapel, which to my surprise I found open. There were coffin-shaped slabs to the memory of John Evelyn who died in 1705 in the 86th year of his life and to Mary Evelyn his wife who died in her 74th year three years later. From these stones I learnt that many of Evelyn's sons died in infancy and that his wife was a model of virtue. There were many other Evelyn monuments, one of them of a John Evelyn who died in 1603. He was the father of 24 children. I saw several brasses on the floor.

On leaving the church I crossed the road at the back of the Wotton Hatch Hotel and found a footpath that led me into the drive of Wotton House, the home of John Evelyn. After passing a wood I came to two gardeners' cottages on the right and a big walled garden. The drive made a half-circle round the edge of a rough field at the end of which I came to the beautifully wooded valley where stands the famous house embowered among the trees that Evelyn was so rightly proud of.

The gardens were adorned with many grottoes and waterways and there was a good deal of statuary standing in niches of the rocks. There were sweet-smelling exotic

[*Photo: Will F. Taylor*

WOTTON, LOOKING TOWARDS N. DOWNS

flowers, but like so many country-houses and parks that had been requisitioned by the Army during the War the whole demesne wore a sad look and I shuddered to think what John Evelyn would have had to say about the condition in which it had been left. But this park is still well worth a visit for, in spite of the ravages of our time, Wotton is still, as it was in his day, "sweetly environed by delicious streams and venerable woods."

After wandering all round the Park which was completely deserted, I retraced my steps up the drive to catch a bus to Dorking from the Wotton Hatch Hotel.

I had walked in all about ten miles.

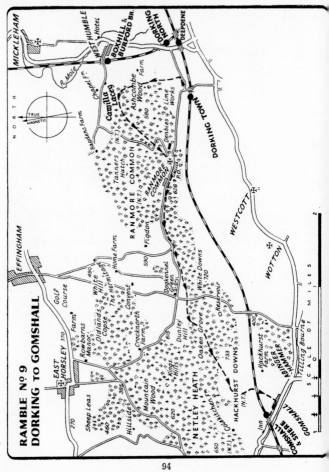

RAMBLE Nº 9
DORKING TO GOMSHALL

RAMBLE 9

Dorking, Ashcombe Wood, Ranmore Common, Dog Kennel Green, Oaken Grove, Hackhurst Downs, Gomshall

INSTEAD of climbing straight out of Dorking directly on to Ranmore I found an enchanting track which led out of a lane going northwards a few hundred yards to the east of Dorking Town station.

This track followed along the western edge of a very large open field with a magnificent view over the whole valley to Box Hill. At the end of the field the track crossed a copse and then a couple of drives after which I found myself in the thick woods of Ashcombe with eating chestnuts, pines and tall oaks. The way led northward along rising ground and at the top the track became indistinct for the deep descent on the other side. But it doesn't matter which way you go down for at the bottom you are bound to strike the very clearly defined woodland track going westward. This climbs gradually out of the gully and curves round to emerge on Ranmore Common close to the post office. Here the common is a wide plateau with an open road running between two very wide grass verges and tracks going off into the woods northwards every few yards. I followed this wide green verge until I came to a cross-roads at Dog Kennel Green. Here I left the road and took the green track that went off south and then veered quickly west. This track is shaded by trees and crosses two other tracks going north and south. When I came to a clearing I veered left along a cart-track that had been sadly churned up by the Army. I came to rest under a tall beech tree where a woodpecker was in a terrible state of agitation. Three girl riders came ambling under the trees. They were the only people I encountered during the whole of my walk. At the edge of Oaken Wood I turned away left past piled up pit-props and came to a gigantic tree all blasted and torn. I then bore left through an ancient grove and turned right along a well-defined track which brought me out on to the brow of the hill at Hackhurst Downs where I lost all count of time as I lay among the beds of whortleberries and wild strawberries and reaped the richest harvest of the latter that I have ever gleaned. Below me lay the railway and I watched the train silently gliding past Hackhurst Farm far below. I was surrounded by myriads of multi-coloured wild flowers and surfeited with wild strawberries.

There was a wide view of the woodland to the south leading to Leith Hill. The flowers shone golden in the dazzling white chalk. The air was scented with wild thyme. There was a glorious profusion of willow-herb and honeysuckle among which saffron and blue butterflies played. It was indeed flaming June at its loveliest.

The descent to Gomshall was steep but the white chalk track obvious. At the foot of the hill the track runs into a

THE COMPASSES INN, GOMSHALL.

lane and where this runs into the main road I turned right towards the railway bridge. The Black Horse was shut, but fifty yards further on I came to the Compasses, a Surrey Public Trust house on the banks of the Tilling-bourne where my enjoyment of the tea on the lawn was enhanced by the presence of ducks on the clear shallow rippling stream and of wagtails and thrushes and robins pecking for crumbs right under my feet.

The station for the train back to Dorking is quite close to the hotel. This walk is between eight and nine miles long.

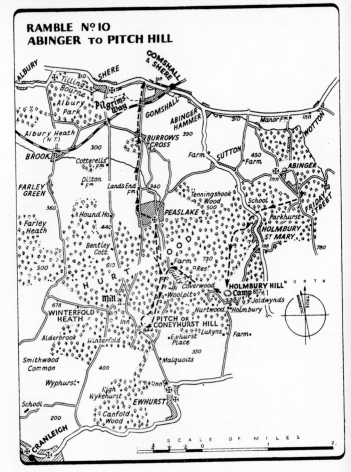

RAMBLE No. 10
ABINGER to PITCH HILL

SCALE OF MILES
½   ¼   0   1   2.

RAMBLE 10

Abinger, Holmbury Hill, Hurt Wood, Pitch Hill, Peaslake

THE Surrey peaks seem to run in threes. Hascombe, Hydon's Ball and Hambledon form one group, and Leith Hill, Holmbury Hill and Pitch Hill (or Coneyhurst as it is printed on the Ordnance Maps) form another, but whereas you can easily take in the former group in a day's walk, I find the latter three too much of a switchback, and there is the added handicap (if it is a handicap) of being lost in Hurt Wood which is so riddled with tracks that even with a compass you are apt to get off the course.

I began this excursion by taking a bus from Dorking to Abinger where I got off at the triangular green.

You will find most of the walkers who get off here turn eastward, for it is the easy and shortest way to Friday Street, but turning westward over the green I passed through a kissing-gate into a fenced path. This led to a wide sandy track and very soon I found myself looking down into and across a fine wooded gorge through which ran a road with many brick houses. This is Holmbury St. Mary.

I crossed the road and took a very steep track up into the opposite woodland where I found an infinite number of tracks, but by keeping more or less due south I eventually

[*Photo: Donovan E. H. Box*

PART OF HOLMBURY ST. MARY

100

came out of the woods on to a clearing where I was soon on the summit of Holmbury Hill which stands 857 feet above the sea. If you look around you can see the remains of a Stone Age camp. You can also see, indeed you can scarcely miss, a view which rivals that from Leith Hill, for the vista extends northward over the tops of the trees to the whole ridge of the North Downs and southward over the weald to the South Downs.

The trouble about Holmbury is that you are likely to feel a strong temptation to make a point across the deep gully westwards to climb Pitch Hill. It looks fairly simple but it isn't. The best way is to go on a little way westwards and then take one of the tracks striking northward for the depths of Hurt Wood. I more or less felt my way, edging always a little north of west until I came to a track which crossed it going due west. I took this, and it brought me out on top of the gully where it had narrowed to a small defile with a road running through the bottom and a farm in the hollow. I crossed at the farm and then climbed the opposite side of the wood where I found a straight track going south that led through more woods until I came out to a clearing at the crest of Pitch Hill. The clearing here is small, about the size of a golf green. On the west stands an old windmill on the other side of another gully. I am not going to enter into an argument as to which of the three peaks provides the widest or loveliest view. The point is that they all well repay the search to find them. You cannot really get lost for long as there is a direct road running north and south through the very heart of Hurt Wood, but

[*Photo: Donovan E. H. Box*

WINDMILL, HURT WOOD

on this occasion I took as few risks as possible. After wandering round the crest of Pitch Hill I took the same northward track that I had come by into the depths of the wood until I came to the top of the gully where the farm lies. But instead of crossing the gully I kept straight along the top parallel to the road and within a mile or so came out at Peaslake.

Peaslake is an old straggling village with a whole medley of roads and tracks leading into and off it. It stands on the very edge of the forest, and after a day's walking in woodland rides without meeting a living creature it seems quite a town. It boasts an unexpectedly large hotel and what was more important from my point of view, a bus service, for after the loveliness of the forest the walk on by way of Burrows Cross to Gomshall is dull.

If it is a choice between walking along a road or taking a bus I now invariably take a bus. So I put off having tea until I was put down at the Compasses at Gomshall where I knew I should get a good meal and be near the station.

This walk is about eight miles if you don't get lost, but it seems much more owing to the labyrinthine tracks of Hurt Wood.

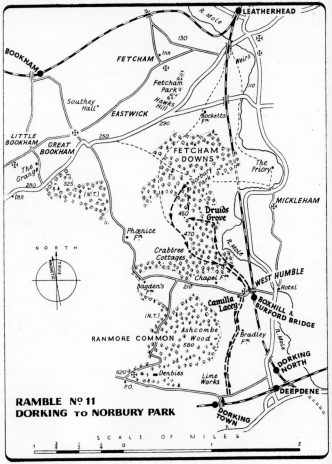

RAMBLE Nº 11
DORKING TO NORBURY PARK

SCALE OF MILES

RAMBLE 11

Dorking, Box Hill Station, Camilla Lacey, Norbury Park, Druid's Grove, Box Hill

I SET out along the chalk track that goes off northward a few hundred yards east of Dorking Town station. At a fork to the right in the great field I turned across the field by Bradley Farm and continued by the field-path which joins the Camilla Lacey road near Box Hill station. Just to the west of the station over the bridge and at the archway of the big house of Leladene, I turned right past St. Michael's chapel along a lane which I followed until I came to a gate with white posts which I entered. This led me to a wide woodland track where I kept right-handed and low down with views over the valley towards Box Hill. The wood was alive with rabbits and squirrels and the beech trees were gigantic. At the foot of the hill is the Druid's Grove, a place of gigantic and curiously shaped yew trees. After passing these I left the track to work my way up left-handed to the top of the hill. The way is well-defined but steep. At the top I found a fence with a track running alongside. I crossed this track and keeping the fence on my left continued my climb till I came out on an open space with a superb view of Mickleham Common,

[Photo: H. D. Keilor

ON BOX HILL, NEAR DORKING

and of Dorking spire. Northward I could see Leatherhead church. I turned back into the wood and keeping on the north side of the fence crossed the drive of Norbury Park (the house of Dr. Marie Stopes) and passing the back of the house I came to an astonishing field of twelve acres of barley all standing, in this first week in June, higher than my head. There is a track through this barley field to Bookham, but I kept to the left of it and came to a signpost marked "Roaring House Farm," where I met a young girl leading a flock of nanny-goats and their kids.

I kept to the middle track here past a tree whose branches were like a ballet dancer on tiptoe with arms extended high over her head.

Eventually I came to a fence where I turned left along a narrow track to another fence which I crossed to join a drive where I turned right and keeping up the hill, joined the lane that led me back through the woods to Box Hill station and the field-path to Dorking by way of Bradley Farm.

This is a very varied ramble of about six miles, one that will specially appeal to the lover of unusual trees.

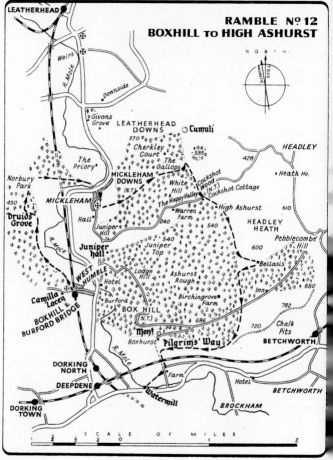

NORTH

TRUE
MAGNETIC

LEATHERHEAD

Weirs

R. Mole

Downside

Givons
Grove

LEATHERHEAD
DOWNS

Cumuli

HEADLEY

The
Priory

370

Cherkley
Court

595

420

Heath Ho.

Norbury
Park

The Gallops

450

MICKLEHAM
DOWNS
(N.T.)

White
Hill

Cockshot
Wood
(N.T.)

Cockshot Cottage

MICKLEHAM

The Happy Valley

High Ashurst

610

Druids
Grove

Hall

Warren
Farm

HEADLEY
HEATH

R. Mole

Juniper
Hill

240

540

600

Pebblecombe
Hill

Juniper
Hall

540

Juniper
Top

Bellasis

WEST
HUMBLE

Lodge
Hill

Hotel

Ashurst
Rough

Inn

650

Camilla
Lacey

Burford

Birchingrove
Farm

782

BOXHILL
BURFORD BRIDGE

BOX HILL
(N.T.)

686

720

Chalk
Pits

R. Mole

Mont
Boxhurst

Pilgrims' Way

BETCHWORTH

DORKING
NORTH

Farm

Hotel

DEEPDENE

Watermill

BETCHWORTH

DORKING
TOWN

BROCKHAM

SCALE   OF   MILES
1   3   1   0   1   2
2   4   4

RAMBLE 12

Mickleham, the Happy Valley, Cockshot Hill, High Ashurst, Birchingrove Farm, Boxhurst, Dorking

WE took the chalk lane that passes the back of the King William IV inn at Mickleham and climbed the Downs in a north-easterly direction.

We crossed the road at the top, turning half-right through a swing-gate that led into a track. This path took us through a wood of yews and we kept straight up avoiding the temptation to veer left. There was a beech wood at the top with tracks going off to the right. But we kept straight on along the track which is signposted "Bridle-Path" in many places and leads straight out on to The Gallops, a fine open grassy expanse about half a mile long.

We kept along the left edge of The Gallops until we came to the far (north) end. I noticed a large number of abnormal sized snails which I felt should be edible. The Gallops are about 100 yards or 150 yards wide and fringed by a dense wind-brake of tall trees on the western side, an admirable place for exercising horses and getting an uninterrupted fast gallop.

At the far end of White Hill the track veered off diagonally right-handed and after following this to the gate

[Photo: Donovan E. H. Box

MICKLEHAM CHURCH

at the end of The Gallops I saw another track descending steeply into what I took to be the Happy Valley. There were wonderful glimpses through the trees over the deep wooded hollow. There was a strong scent of sweetbrier as we descended further into the steep hollow and we often stopped to pick wild strawberries which were larger and more tasteful than I have ever known them before.

At the foot of the slope we came to a road running at right-angles and a cottage called Cockshot Cottage. There was a National Trust signpost showing that we had come through Cockshot Wood. I felt that there should have been another posted at the top of The Gallops where the woods began. There was also a signpost pointing up the track on the further side of the road which read "Box Hill 1¾ miles, Brockham 2¾." We started to climb this by way

110

of an enormous copper beech and soon came to a big brick house on the hilltop. We passed round the wall of this house which was deserted (its name is High Ashurst) and came out on the drive which ran straight along the top of the downland and had a wide margin covered with thorn trees and wild roses. On the right of the road we passed a heavily wired prisoners-of-war camp and on the left we looked out over the wild plateau of Headley Heath.

We soon came to another large brick house, Bellasis, which was being redecorated. Then we came to a colony

[*Photo: H. D. Keilor*

DORKING—THE RIVER MOLE

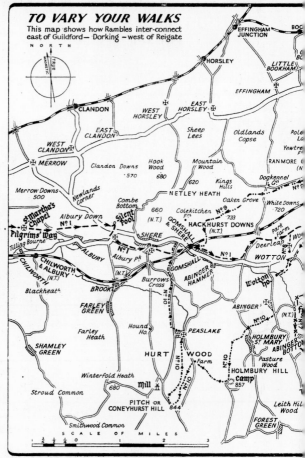

TO VARY YOUR WALKS

This map shows how Rambles inter-connect
east of Guildford — Dorking — west of Reigate

NORTH

TRUE MAGNETIC

EFFINGHAM JUNCTION

BOC

HORSLEY

LITTLE BOOKHAM

BC

CLANDON

WEST HORSLEY

EFFINGHAM

EAST CLANDON

Sheep Lees

Oldlands Copse

Pole La

WEST CLANDON

Yewtre F

MERROW

Clandon Downs · 570

Hook Wood 680

Mountain Wood

RANMORE (N

Merrow Downs 500

Newlands Corner

Kings Hills

620

Dogkennel Co.

No

Combe Bottom

NETLEY HEATH

Oaken Grove

White Downs 720

St. Martha's Chapel

Albury Down

No 1

Silent Pool

660 (N.T.)

Colekitchen Fm

733

HACKHURST DOWNS (N.T.)

Pilgrims' Way

GOMSHALL & SHERE

Tilling Bourne

SHERE

Park Farm

Deerleap

WO

CHILWORTH & ALBURY

ALBURY

No 1

Albury Pk.

No 1

GOMSHALL

No 1

WOTTON

Blackheath

(N.T.)

BROOK

Burrows Cross

ABINGER HAMMER

Wotton Ho.

FARLEY GREEN

Hound Ho.

PEASLAKE

ABINGER

No 10

(N.T.)

f

SHAMLEY GREEN

Farley Heath

HURT WOOD

No 10

Farm

HOLMBURY ST. MARY

BOTTO

ABINGE

Winterfold Heath 680

No 10

No 10

Pasture Wood

HOLMBURY HILL

Mill

Camp 857

Stroud Common

PITCH OR CONEYHURST HILL

844

Leith Hill Wood

Smithwood Common

FOREST GREEN

SCALE OF MILES

½ 0 1 2 3

112

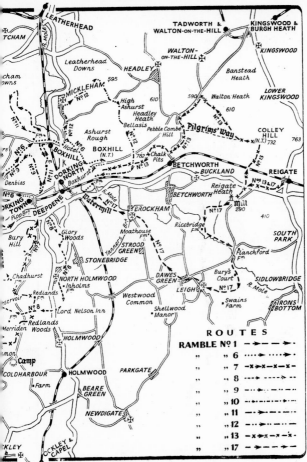

ROUTES

RAMBLE	Nº 1	- → - → - →
,,	,, 6	→ → → →
,,	,, 7	-×-→-×-×-
,,	,, 8	-×→×→×→
,,	,, 9	-----------
,,	,, 10	- - - - -
,,	,, 11	....
,,	,, 12	-·-·-·-·
,,	,, 13	-×-×-×-×-
,,	,, 17	- → - → - →

113

[*Photo : H. D. Keilor*

A SURREY SCENE—GIPSIES ON THE DOWNS

of bungalows and caravans hidden among the trees near Birchingrove Farm.

Here we crossed a road and kept straight along the bridle-track which passed more caravans and tents in fields on the left.

We were soon on the south edge of the escarpment looking right over the wood to Chanctonbury Ring in the distance and Brockham Green at our feet. The vast chalk-pits lay immediately to our left and the track lay steeply in front of us leading down to the valley. We lay for some time on the summit listening to the larks before going down to join the avenue of old yew trees on the right which marked the Pilgrims' Way.

About half a mile along the way was blocked, but by climbing a few hundred feet to the right we were able to skirt the field and regain the Pilgrims' Way as it descended diagonally below Box Hill to Boxhurst where we entered the lane that crossed the railway and then took the foot-path on the right that led us back to Dorking by way of the old water-mill. This walk is about seven miles in all.

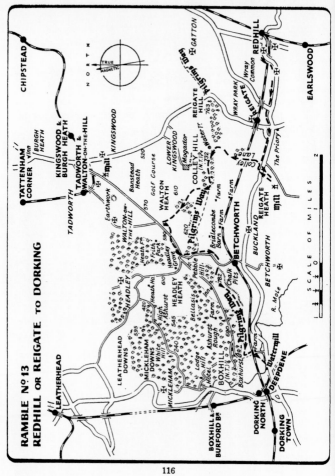

RAMBLE Nº 13
REDHILL OR REIGATE TO DORKING

Reigate, Colley Hill, Walton Heath, Pebble Hill, Pilgrims' Way, Dorking

FOR sixteen consecutive and memorable weeks, walking suddenly became impossible. Days of heavy rain were followed by the severest snowstorms and fiercest frosts within living memory. Then came the floods, and after the floods the gales. Our memory of unhappy days is happily short-lived, but few will forget the first four months of 1947.

It was early May before the ground underfoot became walkable and the countryside was looking as fresh and green as only the English countryside can look in spring as I set out that May morning from Redhill.

I first made a bee-line for Reigate Common, an unspoilt medley of thicket, gorse and bracken with green ways going off in all directions.

Conspicuous on a knoll in mid-common is one of the most interesting windmills in the country. It is a black round "post" windmill with two sweeps, a most picturesque landmark, but not only a landmark, but at some time in its history a church.

There are plenty of windmills converted into dwelling

[*Photo: Donovan E. H. Box*

WINDMILL, REIGATE HEATH

houses, but this is the only instance in the country of a windmill converted into a church.

Its circular round dome is rather like the church of the Holy Sepulchre in Jerusalem on a small scale, the huge wooden centre-post of the mill resting on wooden cross-beams supported on brick plinths decorated with angels.

Just opposite the Black Horse on the north-east edge of Reigate Heath is a lane called Colley Lane which runs more or less direct to the top of Colley Hill. It is signposted. It is a pleasant high-banked affair shaded with tall pines until you come to a house called Pine End which is well named, for it is at this point that you pass out of the sand-stone (on which the pine flourishes) into the chalk where no pine grows.

I found my first bluebell of the season in the small banks of this lane which was thick with the largest violets I have seen for years. Just beyond the Manor House the lane veers to the right. The road straight ahead is private. I came to a cement track on the left also signposted and this was succeeded by a very pleasant way made of thousands of discarded railway sleepers which brought me to the foot of the hill. Here I encountered my first walkers of the day, a boy in white silk shirt open at the neck, and a pretty girl in red and white with her stockingless legs so pale that I imagined that she, like me, was taking her first walk of the year.

After passing a chalk-pit the way splits up into four. I chose the right-hand track and then foolishly left it in my eagerness to scramble up Colley Hill at its steepest angle.

This brought its deserved reward, my only mishap of the day. After I had traversed about half the steep slope I sat down to have a look at the view, and sat heavily on my glasses. That was the end of that. Mercily I still had my field-glasses, which I now brought out to scan the southern horizon, and though it was too dim to see the Shoreham Gap, Chanctonbury Ring was, as I expected, clearly visible.

It was the best possible kind of walking day. There was a fresh south-west wind, quite a lot of blue sky and sunshine, and a fair sprinkling of scurrying cloud. After about two rests I attained the granite monument on the summit to the memory of the soldier George Simpson of the Royal West Surrey Regiment who was killed in the 1914-1918 War. It had been erected by his mother to commemorate that fact and the fact that she had given that section of Colley Hill to the nation in his memory. This gift of a lovely tract of ground is surely by far the most worthy as it is the most lasting memorial we can make to those who gave their lives that the land should remain free.

Colley Hill is less well-known than Leith Hill or Box Hill. In my opinion it outshines them both. It is more open. The view is even more extensive. It is less frequented. The summit of the hill is higher, reached by crossing a viaduct above a chalk-pit and climbing some steps. It is crowned not by the ugly brick water tower which is so conspicuous from the weald, but by a very remarkable covered drinking fountain which looks like a miniature Greek temple. This was erected by R. W. Inglis in 1909, and presented to the corporation of Reigate. Its roof, decorated with a

[*Photo: H. D. Keilor*

COLLEY HILL

flamboyant mosaic in which are represented the signs of the zodiac, is supported by twelve pillars and contains on one side a fountain, and on the other, a plaque containing a coat of arms and the motto *"Never wonne ne never shall,"* which strikes me as very appropriate for this scene.

A heavy leaden cup is supplied for wayfarers to slake their thirst. I for one was grateful for the happy thought. After the climb I was ready for a drink, and the pure chalk water was as welcome as nectar.

There are two notices near the fountain. One is to warn cyclists off and the other instructing visitors to keep to the right. The open, close-cropped wide sward is for walkers. There were four people seated on a bench, but they looked too fat and well dressed for anything but motorists. I saw no road, but suspected its presence. There was only one walker and he was heavily overcoated and accompanied by a dog. I suspected him of living in one of the many rich-looking houses that lie embowered among trees just below the crest of the hill.

I began my walk westwards with the tower of Leith Hill and the whole rich dark green sweetness of the weald unrolled below me. On the face of it you would think it a simple matter just to keep on the crest of the escarpment as the ancient pilgrims did all the way to Dorking.

It is not, alas, simple at all. I wanted a view all the way, the sun and wind in my face and the springy downland turf under my feet.

Next time I shall keep to the southern part of the hill where, I believe, the track is well marked. On this occasion having with difficulty gained the heights, I meant to keep on them. At first the way was easy. It led past the ugly water tower, and then veered off right-handed towards Walton Heath. I didn't want the Heath. I wanted the crest of the escarpment, so at the first opportunity I turned left down a short lane which led to the gates of a large country house. Just outside these gates is a very narrow path lying between fences. I followed this. The fence on my left was a neat affair of green camouflage net. I crossed a drive to another narrow twitten with great gardens and fine houses on either side of the track. There were two white houses, one called Mouse Hill, where the track widened and then narrowed again to lead me through a wet and very ancient wood. This felt like the Pilgrims' Way and I'm pretty sure it was.

I came to a parting of the ways, one track leading steeply down left-handed, the other to wind round a most curious dell with a knoll in it crowned with beech trees that looked to me like a prehistoric burial ground. Unfortunately the way to the wood is barred with fences and barbed wire and the track turns north.

There is apparently no escape from Walton Heath. It is a very good heath, a wild medley of gorse and bracken, and in the distance I saw the spire of what I took to be Tadworth church, but my objective was the west, so I kept going along the edge of a high flint wall until I was stopped again at the entrance to Walton Oaks which was a Canadian Army Depot in the War and is now being converted into an Agricultural College. Here I was again driven northwards until I joined the high road going north and south. Just south of where I joined it I saw two bridle-path notices. The one on the right pointed the way to Headley, the one on the left to Buckland. I did not want either, I wanted a chalk track to Dorking.

I walked south along the unhedged road until I came to a toll-house and a fork. The right-hand road seems the obvious one. It keeps on the top and leads straight to Box Hill. However, I know of old that this road leads to houses and trees, and I wanted open country, so I took the less obvious route, the steep descent to the south. About two-thirds of the way down the hill which is very steep indeed, I came to a hamlet standing on the outskirts of an immense chalk-pit and cement works. I took the right-handed lane that climbs up the hill again and then almost immediately turned left again past some cottages and I saw ahead the white chalk track leading westward. This track crosses a bridge with the works on the left and the chalk-pit on the right. The vast quarry is disused and is now gaily decorated with fresh young trees. I loitered on the bridge for a long time to watch a young girl in a nearby field schooling a very restive but extremely handsome chestnut with white fetlocks. I suspected that she was putting him through his paces for the Surrey Union Point-to-Point which was to take place at Charlwood on the following Saturday. The shades of Jorrocks are not yet dead in Surrey.

To my surprise I found that my very delectable track, instead of keeping alongside the downs as I expected, was winding well up again to skirt the edge of yet another hill. Soon I was again on the summit of the downs in a wood of extraordinarily shaped ancient yews and thorns. On my right and not sufficiently hidden were a number of unsightly shacks and caravans, the refuse from which had been tipped into the ancient wood.

The track is narrow and winds in and out of the wood, through a good deal of tangled undergrowth.

I found myself again brought to a halt by a forbidding high flint wall and had to drop down once more through the wood, where I had the sense not to be lured by a broad track going upwards again, but took the lower broad track which was unmistakably the Pilgrims' Way. This brought me well into open country with a full view of Dorking and the spire of Ranmore church directly in front of me.

At Boxhurst I turned south down the footpath to the lane that led me over the railway and where the road on the left came in I climbed the steps to the stile on the right that led me on to a footpath that crossed a few fields and then brought me over the river to join the main road just above the old mill.

I should describe this walk, which is about twelve miles and took me five hours, as one of varied enchantment. It has three distinct stages. The first stage, climbing to and roaming over Colley Hill is pure enchantment. The road that cuts down the gully is not only dull, it is also dangerous. Motorists, I find, resent footsloggers more than ever since the War. The third stage along the sides of the chalk-pits within full view of the world is again pure enchantment, and as variety is the spice of life, I think you will find this walk, as I found it, immensely enjoyable. It is about twelve or thirteen miles in all.

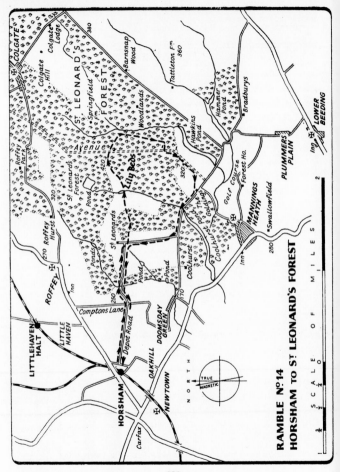

RAMBLE Nº 14
HORSHAM TO ST LEONARD'S FOREST

Horsham, St. Leonard's Forest, Lily Beds, The Goldings, Coolhurst, Horsham

ONE great advantage of this walk is that you touch no main roads and are in the forest pretty well from start to finish. Horsham is a town not only of great historic interest but also of considerable architectural beauty, so before you set out for the forest you should make your way south from the station to see the church, the ancient meeting of the four ways at Carfax and the old posting-house of the Black Horse inn.

The forest walk however begins, as I said, at the station. I crossed over the bridge that spans the platforms eastward and almost at once turned left at the Bedford Hotel opposite a most unexpected old Sussex farmhouse with tall chimney and Horsham stone roofing.

After about a hundred yards along this road I turned right-handed up Depot Road which began by being a town street of relatively modern small villas and then after the allotments imperceptibly changed its nature and became a quiet country-hedged lane. This led me to Compton's Lane which is signposted and ran left and right. I crossed this into a sandy lane with a big modern timber and brick house on my left and then went down into forest glades with bracken, bushes and pine trees on both sides of the now open woods. There was a track going off to the

WINTER LOVELINESS—HORSHAM, THE CAUSFWAY

left to Roffey and a track going off right to Coolhurst, but I kept straight on along the lane with strong smelling bay trees and a high deer fence on my left and open woodland on my right.

At the top of the hill I came to a cross-road. The left-hand track led through a white gate painted "Private to St. Leonards"; the right-hand became an avenue leading to Coolhurst.

A little to the right I came to a kissing-gate leading into a very narrow "twitten" going off to the left. By mistake I took this until I came to a group of cottages where, to my surprise, I found someone to put me on the right track. If I had gone straight on, I should have come to Roffey. There was no way directly over the fields, so I went back to the kissing-gate and found that the track I wanted turned in just a few yards south of the gate where I went wrong.

In other words, when you get to the avenue leading to St. Leonards, turn right-handed and take the second kissing-gate on the left. It is just after you pass a small pond. The way east is clearly marked by a green track running along a left-hand fence lined with laurels with an open field on the right. I passed through stout wooden gates and came to a thick oak post with a gamekeeper's cottage on the left. Then I entered the forest proper. The path led me across a track which led out into the open on the right by barn stacks, and after crossing this track my way suddenly widened out into a many-furrowed bridle-track which narrowed as I dropped down a steep gully of beech woods, with heather growing in great profusion. This led me down to the strange low-lying land of the lily beds. The tradition is that when St. Leonard was murdered, each drop of blood that fell became the breeding ground of wild lilies of the valley for ever after.

The forest is very thick here and the narrow path follows the left side of a deep gully crossing over on the right side of a trickling stream. The wind made a pleasant sighing noise in the creaking trees up the boughs of which grey and black squirrels scampered by the score. Within one minute I put up one very noisy cock pheasant, almost trod on a too silent adder which took no trouble to get out of my way and nearly fell over a baby rabbit.

I was in the very heart of the forest. Then on the crest of the hill I came to the fine broad avenue which cuts right through the forest from Faygate to Mannings Heath.

If you want to keep to the broad wide forest track you will be wise to turn to the right here. I'll join you later.

I crossed this main broadway and my track immediately deteriorated. It veered off half-right, and then I came to a notice which read "Danger—Rifle Range," but it seemed unlikely that there could have been any danger for several years, so I plunged on through the trees down a very steep slope hoping to find a clearing at the foot of the ravine. What I did find was my way blocked forward but a track going off on the right alongside a fence. I took this and then began a battle for about an hour with bracken that grew well over my head. Eventually I fought my way through to a track coming downhill to meet my path. I turned right-handed up this track for a little way until I found myself once more in the fine stately broad avenue that I advised you to follow if you wanted a safe walk. I turned south along this until I came to open country and a gate where I put up two brace of hen pheasants.

Soon after I saw an immensely fine clump of trees in a field on my right, so I took the track on my right leading me along the southern edge of this field. This gave me a fine view of the Mannings Heath golf course, on the other side of a little stream-fed valley.

I came out in the lane leading to Doomsday Green at the farm known as The Goldings where I found a most attractive hedgeless road with paths going off into the forest on my right and then to the banks of the narrow, long Coolhurst Hammer Pond on my left.

I wandered down to this lovely sheet of silent forest lake and spent some time walking round its banks before returning to the Doomsday Green road which I deserted on coming to the lodge gates of St. Leonards. There is a track going right-handed just before you come to the lodge gates, so make sure you are at the lodge before you turn right. The track here comes in from the south, crosses the road and goes up the sandy avenue towards the big house. This is where I turned in and after about a mile I had completed my circuit by coming again to the kissing-gate where I had turned in before. The way back to Horsham is along the footpath that I have already described.

This walk took me about four hours and the distance I covered was about eight miles. If you like woodland walks in absolute quietude you will find St. Leonard's forest ideal.

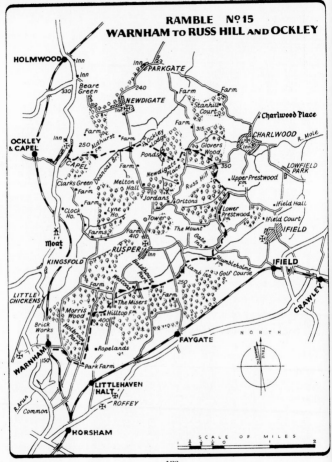

HOLMWOOD

Inn

Inn

Beare
Green

330

Inn
PARKGATE

240

NEWDIGATE

Inn

Farm

Farm

Stanhill
Court

Charlwood Place

OCKLEY
& CAPEL

Inn

250

Aldhurst

Farm

Ockley
Lodge

Ponds

315

Glovers
Wood

CHARLWOOD

Inn

R. Mole

LOWFIELD
PARK

CAPEL

Denoak Br.

Farm

Newdigate
Place

350

Russ Hill

Upper Prestwood
Fm

Clarks Green

Farm

Melton
Hall

Jordans

Orltons

Lower
Prestwood
Fm

Ifield Hall

Ifield Court

IFIELD

Clock
Ho.

Farm

Lyne
Ho.

Farms

Tower

Farm
410

The Mount

Gate
Inn

Moat

KINGSFOLD

RUSPER

Inn

Stumbleholms
Golf Course

IFIELD

LITTLE
CHICKENS

Babinonite
Place

Farm

Westons

The Misers

Farm

Lamb Inn

250

CRAWLEY

Brick
Works

Morris
Wood

Holbrook Park

Hilltop Fm
400

WARNHAM

150

Ropelands

Park Farm

FAYGATE

NORTH

TRUE
MAGNETIC

LITTLEHAVEN
HALT

ROFFEY

R. Arun

Common

HORSHAM

SCALE OF MILES

Warnham, Holbrook Park, Morris Wood, The Misers, Baldhouse Park, Lamb's Green, Stumbleholme Farm, The Mount, Lower Prestwood Farm, Russ Hill, Glover's Wood, Newdigate Place, Ockley Lodge, Tanthouse Farm, Aldhurst Farm, Capel, Ockley Station

I HAD a quite perfect cloudless day in late September for this most exciting walk through the woods and over the fields of the Surrey-Sussex border. It was exciting because most of the fields had lost all but the barest trace of the tracks so clearly outlined on the Ordnance Survey Map while the woods were so intersected with tracks not marked on the map that even with constant reference to the compass it was difficult not to lose my sense of direction.

I left the train at Warnham and took the lane going directly east which led into a lane where I turned right-handed to make a circuit round Holbrook Park which lay on my left. At the south-eastern edge of the path I took the lane leading steeply northward up the hill past Repelands on my right, a brick house with a curious medley of medieval brick chimneys, and the grey mansion of Holbrook Park on my left. This is a surprisingly large

WARNHAM CHURCH

[Photo: H. D. Keilor

country-house to be placed so near a road. You would expect to find it in the centre of a demesne of ten thousand acres.

Overlooking it, standing superbly on the crest of the hill, stood a much more attractive brick house with a view commanding, without any interruption, the whole sweep of the Sussex Weald to Chanctonbury and the Devil's Dyke. This many-windowed happy-looking house is called Morris Wood and less than fifty yards beyond the opening of its drive stands the very unobstrusive grey gate which leads into the first of the woods in which I spent the

THE VILLAGE STREET, WARNHAM [*Photo : H. D. Keilor*

greater part of the day. This gate is on the right-hand side of the road. Immediately I was among tall pines along the boughs of which squirrels were racing in their dozens. If you look on the map you will see only one track marked in this wood, going off north-east but I soon came to a fork where I turned left and then bore right through a very lovely glade. There were more and more tracks to choose from, but I bore left up a rough ride, crossed a bridge with a field on my left, bore right again and eventually came out on a road where I turned left. Soon I came to The Misers, originally the name of an inn that stood here. Now there are only two cottages and there was as usual no human being within hail. There was washing hanging out and dogs barked but I couldn't find anyone to direct me. A slight rise in the road followed and then a road came in from the left and almost immediately I saw a stile on the right but no sign of the footpath so clearly marked on the map. On the other hand in mid-field I saw a lonely stout stile standing in complete isolation and at the further end of the field I saw a gap.

As I crossed the field towards the lonely stile I saw that there was a faint tinge of a different coloured green to show where the track originally ran. There was a big yellow house on the left and fine views of the woods to the south. I passed through the gap in the far end of the field and came to another field with a big farm with ricks decorated with little twisted ornaments of straw on the top. This was a lovely house with trim lawns and fine orchards. Its name was Westons. I passed along down the side of the drive to the lodge gates and emerged into a road which I crossed to enter a gate which led along a broad ridgeway with ten ricks in a row. There was a big house on the left and a well cared for park on the north side of a rise. This was Baldhouse Park.

I passed over a gate and kept along a track on the left edge of a field with a big wood on the right. This led me past a group of crab-apple trees over another gate into a field in which there was a herd of picturesque white-polled cattle with black ears.

I then crossed over on to the other side of the hedge and turned half-left across a field towards a lane leading from a large red house in the dip on the left. This led me out on to a road with a medieval brick house with fine lawns on the right.

A signpost on the road running east read "Lamb's Green," a place not mentioned on the map. This lane was remarkable for the number of strange archways and gateways that the houses boasted. There was in particular a four-square brick skeleton of a gazebo in front of a brick house. The local architects seemed to have had a lot of fun experimenting here. An ancient tree trunk in a field looked exactly like some prehistoric dinosaur. The lane was wide margined and goats were grazing all the way along.

Then followed a number of brick cottages and to my surprise, as it wasn't mentioned on the map, I came to the Lamb inn bearing an attractive sign. I was met at the entrance by two extraordinarily courteous white-haired hostesses who to my astonishment answered my query about food with "I could cut you a double sandwich." "What's inside?" I asked. "Meat" they said in chorus. I nearly fell flat on the floor. There was a girl cyclist in shorts, a chauffeur and a very fat spaniel whose age I was told is eight.

The hostesses reappeared to ask a joint question—"Not a draught for you is there?" they asked gently. The conversation continued on the spaniel's diet and then turned on the closed footpath. "There's a path to Stumbleholme Farm," they said, "but the Canadian soldiers tore down the notice and burnt it and now the Brickworks have blocked up the path. There's a smuggler's lane."

Everyone said that the way on lies through the

CHARLWOOD

Photo: H. D. Keilor

brickyard. It doesn't. Just beyond the brickworks is an over-grown smuggler's track through which I fought my way and eventually found myself at Stumbleholme Farm where I turned north over the stream to rejoin the road just east of the Gate inn where I went to ask about any possible field-path to Russ Hill. The landlord could only recommend the road, so I went back along the road to the east, past a very jolly white house with carriage lamps hanging from the porch.

Then I came to the drive to the Mount where I was very disappointed to find my way barred by a "Private" notice, so I was forced to continue along the lane north-east where I was struck by the uniformity of all the gates. They were all painted green and red and consisted of two iron horizontal poles with strands of wire between them. I took the first road on the left that climbed steeply up the hill and met an elderly man coming down the hill who warned me that the track to Russ Hill might well be piled up with undergrowth. At the top of the hill two men working in a yard added their warning. "You might get through," they said without conviction. From the west of this hill I got a grand view southward of the Sussex Weald. There was a road going off to the left but I kept straight on down into the hollow where at Lower Prestwood Farm there was an obvious field-path cutting off the corner to Russ Hill. It was not marked on the ordnance map, but it is marked on some of the footpaths maps, so if you feel like it I should take it. You can't be in for a harder time than I had. I should have taken this track if I had been able to rouse the people in the farm, but I only roused the dogs.

A little further along the road I met a man building a rick. "You'll need a hatchet to cut your way through to Russ Hill," he said.

The turning came at a brick cottage where the road turned away right. There is a field-path going off half-right which might have been helpful, but the track to Russ Hill is so plainly marked on the map that I meant to take it, hatchet or no hatchet.

I was left in no doubt from the start. The track was obviously once wide enough for horses to ride. It was incredibly overgrown. I fought my way through brambles

[Photo: Donovan E. H. Box

ON FRENSHAM COMMON

for what seemed miles and eventually joined a gully and turned left up a clearing and bore right. It was a blind fight, a long fight and a difficult fight, and after a struggle that I shall not lightly forget I suddenly saw the light of day ahead, came to a clearing and saw above me on the other side of a large field, the tall white towers of the mansion of Russ Hill. When I reached the road by the big house, I saw a notice-board which announced that the house was sold. That surprised me, for it looked as if the Army had left this house in an even worse mess than usual.

There are a number of houses on the hill which provides a grand view northward of Leith Hill, Box Hill and Colley Hill, but the woods hide the view to the south. Just opposite to the entrance to the big house is an unobtrusive track leading across a field right into the heart of Glover's Wood. According to the map there is only one track going north-west, but as soon as you get into the wood you find an infinite number of tracks. I passed down a steep gully north and then found a fine track with nut trees on either side. At broad cross-tracks I turned left which led down and across a wide and deep gully. You will easily recognise this track because it is paved with stones on both sides of the gully.

On the left the country soon opened out and although there were many confusing tracks I kept on moving north-west and after crossing a field of stubble, I reached the road by a red-brick house. This was the lodge to Newdigate Place and I crossed the road to go down the drive which is a right of way. The big red-brick mansion of Newdigate

[Photo: H. D. Keilor

FARM POND AT OCKLEY

Place is deserted. Stags' antlers still decorate the mansion gateway and a curious young tree resembling antlers is growing out of one of the main chimneys. The stained glass in the windows seems miraculously to have escaped damage during the military occupation. The view over the field and woods to Box Hill and Leith Hill from the drive is magnificent.

After passing the house I took the right-hand fork of the drive leading into an immensely long straight avenue of young oaks where a whole line of ammunition dumps now lie derelict.

Then quite without warning I came to two large lakes, one on either side of the avenue. The one on the left is the larger and fuller and contains two little islands between which a boy was punting.

The sun was blazing down. It seemed an ideal resting-place. For half an hour I lay by the side of the upper lake and listened to the plopping of the fish rising and the distant hum of an aeroplane and the firing of big guns. I watched a heron lazily flying above the trees and the usual crowd of scampering squirrels.

Beyond the lakes I came to Ockley Lodge, a handsome farm with tall chimneys and Horsham stone roof built partly of black timber and ancient brick. There was as usual no one about anywhere near the farm.

Next came a large house on the right and eventually I came to the very stout stone lodge and the gates leading into the road. I turned right for a few yards and then crossed the road and turned in left-handed to a gate just

[Photo: H. D. Keilor

THE PICTURESQUE CHURCH AT CAPEL.

before a group of houses and a stream. The track ran along the edge of a ploughed field at the end of which I had to cross a ramshackle old wooden trestle bridge over the brook. On the further side I kept up the ridge half-right to a farmhouse right on the crest made of ancient brick and timber with a Horsham stone roof. Here luckily there was someone at home, a woman sawing wood who gave me most explicit directions. I turned left round the farm and bore right for a couple of fields where there was an unexpected gravel narrow footpath running along the south side of the field.

There was a fine view southward of ridges of woodland. This track brought me out on to the road where I turned right for a few yards and then turned in left again opposite Tanthouse Farm through a gate past a caravan called the Stags which led to a wide track through the woods where men were felling trees. Then it veered diagonally right-handed across a big stubble field and entered a wood where there were the usual confusing criss-crossing tracks. By keeping well to the right and bearing always to the right I came out of the wood into rising ground from the top of which I found myself looking down on to the church spire and red roofs of the compact village of Capel. I came out on the main road at a big farm where the Ayrshire herd were just going in to be milked.

Opposite the church I found a comfortable tea-room and after tea walked down the village street to take the first turn to the right which led me to the station at Ockley.

I was out seven hours and I covered about fifteen miles.

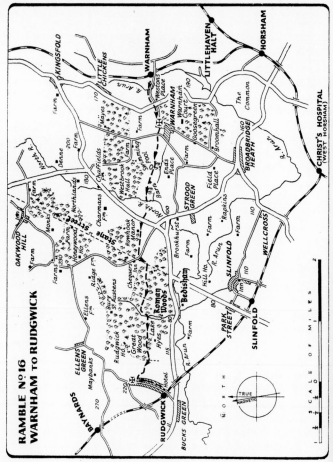

RAMBLE No 16
WARNHAM TO RUDGWICK

Warnham Station, Warnham Village, Bathing Pool, Rowhook Manor, The Chequers, Stane Street, Roman Woods, The Lake, Hyes, Rudgwick

THIS was in many ways the most satisfying of all the cross-country walks that I have taken since the War, because for once the track, in spite of being obviously out of use and frequently barred, is yet clearly visible as a track the whole way. I began this walk from Warnham station where I turned westwards past a row of cottages on the right and after a quarter of a mile came to the main road where I bore left and crossed it to take the lane to Warnham church. There was a good deal of building of council houses going on on my right and on my left was the great park of Warnham Court which like so many other large private houses has been bought by the Govern- for a Civil Service Establishment.

Warnham village is almost hidden under a forest of orchards and its stalwart stone church tower rises from a mass of trees. The churchyard is remarkable for the thickness and symmetry of its shaped yews, the best of which acts as an arch over the lych-gate.

The interior of the church is massive, much too large for the size of the village and unexpectedly light in view of the great number of stained glass windows.

Very tall poplars line one side of the village street which had a single occupant, a policeman standing by the telephone as I came round the corner. He was, I think, the only policeman I have ever met who was knowledgeable about footpaths. It was because he gave me so detailed and graphic a picture that I was never at a loss from the word go. He was standing just opposite the narrow twitten where I turned in. It had a low fenced railing and abutted on the rectory garden on one side and a picturesque brick house with Horsham stone roofing on the other. After one field it led to the very well-kept cricket ground which has a handsome wooden pavilion and large white screens. If anybody still walked I imagine that the cricketers would resent the presence of this right of way running right across the centre of their pitch. A whole new colony of council houses was being built on the rising ground above the cricket pitch and already the footpath has here been absorbed into the road, but only for a few yards, for on coming to another road, crossing it at right-angles, I saw the footpath on the other side leading to a little wood westward. Then came a ploughed field. This was the first ploughed field I have crossed since the War where the footpath across has been left unploughed. It ran, a green little ridgeway as field-paths used to run. It was in my eyes a miracle. Then followed another wood, and again I came to a ploughed field where the green track had been left unscathed. I could hardly believe my eyes. The path ran up a high south-facing slope overlooking a gully. Not quite at the top of the field there was a post and rails to give

the direction, and after negotiating these I came to a plantation on my right, and the path ran down to a gap in the
hedge with a stile and another post and rails. The track
continued clear and green along the south side of the hedge.
It was quite astonishing just to be able to follow one's nose
and not find at each field's end that the opportunist farmer
had piled up impregnable barbed-wire entanglements.

There were fine views of undulating thickly wooded
country and parklands to the south. The trees blocked out
the view to the north.

I came to a very well-hidden smuggler's lane running
north and south which was less overgrown than I expected
to find it. I put up from under my feet a gigantic cock and
a hen pheasant and then crossed the lane to a field with a
newly planted lot of firs. Then I saw on my right a most
astonishing sight, or it would have been astonishing had
the Warnham policeman not warned me to look out for
it—a round enclosure fenced in by high wooden palings.
Peeping through cracks in the fence I caught glimpses of a
huge derelict open-air swimming pool with elaborate
changing rooms. It was obviously built by a private owner
for his own pleasure, but where was his house ? I was in the
very depths of the country and on the top of a hill and I
could see no house at all. I could only conclude after
looking at the map that it must have belonged to Westbrook Hall, but it was a long way to come for a swim in
your own private pool. It was larger than most town
public swimming pools and made me wonder why it had
not been acquired by Warnham for its youth. I forged

ahead, leaving the pool on my right and after passing another plantation came to a tarred barn on my left about which I had also been warned by the policeman. Here there was a Clapham Junction of tracks, but I went steadily onwards west over two fields to a gate, through a plantation and down to a deep ditch or small stream which was spanned by a neat little wooden bridge.

On the further side of the water I got evidence of another type of owner, one who loves wire. Directly across the field from the bridge a stile had been recently rebuilt and I climbed an upland field where I met the first human being I had encountered since parting with the policeman. He told me that he had felled most of the trees in the Roman Woods, so he knew the way there if anybody did, but I disregarded his advice and still kept straight westwards to a stile that led on to the main London-Bognor road. The traffic on this road was tremendous, and I realised more than ever that for the walker there is but one way. If he is to enjoy his walk, see the country, and be free from the fear of sudden death all the time he must keep away from the main highway. As I sat on the stile a man came down the road and stopping said, "It's a long time since I saw anyone sitting on that stile. It used to be our main way to Warnham."

"It was my way from Warnham," I said. He shook his head. He found it difficult to believe that. "They should be compelled to open these paths again," he said, pointing across the road to the top of the field opposite.

"That's the right of way to the Chequers and the Roman Woods," he said.

"That's the way I'm going," I said, and I did.

The way is plainly marked on the map and the track was clearly outlined over the field. So I crossed the road, went through the gate on the further side leaving the lovely brick house of Rowhook Manor on my immediate right and walked up the big field of rising ground to the gap among the trees at the top. There was a stile here and on the further side the track went along the edge of a field of roots and through a plantation to another grass field where a Friesian herd were grazing.

There was a farm on my left and a notable view of Leith Hill northward. Then followed another plantation, then a ploughed field with the track completely ploughed under, but the gap on the further side was plain. I skirted the field left-handed by the farm and came out at the meeting of Stane Street and the road from Ewhurst to Horsham. Two grey horses stood outside the white Chequers inn, which has a fine lamp and an old tree outside. It looked a most fitting place for a meet of hounds and one of the riders told me that it was to be the rendezvous for a cub-hunting meet during the following week. "At 7.30 in the morning," she said. "Not much to drink at that hour," said the white-haired landlord, Mr Harrison, who had come out to see the riders off.

There was the largest pumpkin I have ever seen occupying practically the whole of the handsome and very ancient oak table in the public bar. In a little room a few steps up I saw some more remarkably good antique chairs. The Chequers could not have been more conveniently

THE CHEQUERS INN

[Photo : H. D. Keilor

situated, had it been in the old days, but Mr. Harrison could spare us no food of any sort. There was however beer. He drew a lugubrious picture of the state of the woods beyond. "I rode to the bottom once," he said." Never again."

I didn't at all want to leave the ancient stone flooring, low ceilings and general medieval atmosphere of this very fascinating pub, so I listened to Mr. Harrison joining in the general execration of the farmers for stopping up the rights of way.

"To go down Stane Street to Roman Gate," he said, "you've got to crawl on your hands and knees. With all those woodmen it wouldn't have taken an hour to clear a way, and it's all happened in the last twelve months."

When I left the Chequers I turned immediately right-handed up the narrow lane which is part of the ancient Roman way of Stane Street and was surprised to find quite a colony of little houses and a tiny derelict village school with smashed windows in the woods.

Stane Street itself veers left at the top of the rise and descends steeply south-west to Roman Gate where it again becomes the main London-Chichester road.

My way bore to the right on the top of the hill past a lovely little brick cottage on the left and then became a wide track leading into the heart of the Roman Wood. There is no question about it, these ancient trees, which may or may not have had ancestors standing here when the Romans first climbed up from the southern sea on their way to London, have an atmosphere peculiarly their own. I felt that I had suddenly been pulled back into primeval Britain.

Two German prisoners-of-war coming up from the tree-felling reassured me that I was on my way to the lake. And indeed at first it was easy and obvious for it was the track of the woodcutters. Then I came down to the clearing where there was a very wide track going south and north. I could hear the cutters away to the north, but no other sound. There were suddenly sweet smells for which I couldn't account and a lot of birdsong. There was a bewildering choice of ways, but I kept on westward and finding the woods falling away in front of me knew that I was coming to the valley of the great lake, and all at once

[*Photo: H. D. Keilor*]

"—UP THE NARROW LANE WHICH IS PART OF THE ANCIENT ROMAN WAY OF STANE STREET" (—*but the mud is not always there!*)

I saw it far below. Half a dozen wild-duck got up from the tall bulrushes which fringe its shores. There was a wild outcry of waterfowl and one heron rose up and leisurely flapped its way over my head.

This is a very wide valley and you can cross it only at the top or the bottom. There were paths all round the lake and the tree trunks are well cut with initials. After drinking in the glory of the lake I turned right-handed and found a tiny wooden footbridge hidden among the reeds at the north end. In point of fact this lake is so wild and so lovely that it is well worth walking all round it.

After crossing the bridge I bore left along an avenue of picturesque beech trees and then found that I had to cross another stream by an even smaller wooden bridge. This brought me to the meeting of four ways. I judged the track going half-left to be the appropriate one and I was right, for on the top of the field on my left stood a large red-brick farmhouse which was obviously Hyes. I kept along a shady rutty lane with a deep gully on my right. A good deal of the wood had been felled and one wide track led off to the left towards Hyes where I saw enormous wood piles. Wood piles in England are now of course as common as turf piles in Ireland, but this Hyes collection was calculated to keep the Hyes fires burning and well alight for something like a hundred years.

I avoided taking this left-hand track and kept on going along the edge of the wood, though the going became for the first time a little uncertain. But it brought me out to the end of the great wood at a wooden gate which gave on to a wide green lane. Lying across this lane is a most strange monolith, a great slab of stone looking like a refectory table, about 5 inches thick, 12 feet long and 3 feet broad. I can't think what the purpose of this stone could be, but it made a fitting climax to my Roman Woods experience.

This green lane is almost immediately crossed by another green lane equally wide, equally picturesque and equally wild. On the right was a blacked tarred barn close

SUNSHINE AND SHADOW ON AN OLD CORNER OF RUDGWICK

by a tall chimneyed farm. I crossed this lane to a gate where the green track ran on westwards. From this gate I got a superb view of Blackdown in the distant haze to the west and the ridge of the South Downs nearer and clearer to the south. I went through the gate, leaving the cottage on my right, and passed down the side of the field to a dip with a plantation on the left from which another track came up to join mine. I crossed the stile and found the track marked by a series of stone steps which led me through a plantation up to a ploughed field with the path still clearly defined along the right edge. I climbed up the side of the hill with a house on the right. The path then veered left into a twitten with houses on both sides and then ran parallel with a new drive and ended at a drive gate painted white on the road in Rudgwick village. No indication is given at its unobtrusive entrance and this is a public right of way. It is made to look like a private carriage drive.

Rudgwick is most attractive. Its little church stands on a knoll to the north, and most of the houses are of mellow brick tiles, standing on the west side of the road-way. Many of the roofs and walls are covered with creeper. The builders were extremely busy with new brick houses. I turned south and found hospitality at the Martlets Hotel which stands most conveniently within a few seconds of the railway station where I later caught my train.

One of the remarkable features of this walk is the fact that it is not only absolutely wild all the way, but still clear to see, easy to find and absolutely straight, running east to west with scarcely a deviation. I had covered in all about eight miles.

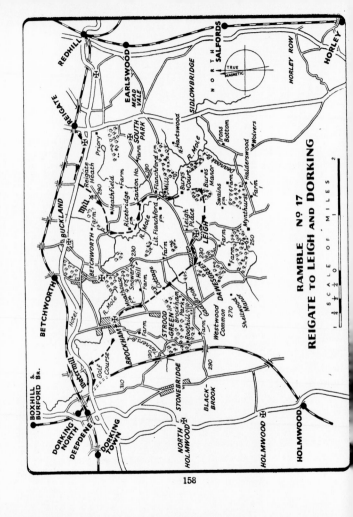

RAMBLE Nº 17
REIGATE TO LEIGH AND DORKING

Reigate, Reigate Heath, Betchworth Mill, The Mole, Ricebridge Farm, Flanchford, Bury's Court, Leigh, Dawes Green, Moat House, Brockham, Betchworth Park, Dorking

FROM the map you would judge this to be a gentle, unadventurous, easy ramble. When I planned it I looked forward to a day meandering along the banks of the Mole and its adjoining water-meadows. It turned out to be one of the most worth-while walks I did, but totally different from anything that I had visualised. I started from Reigate and walked westwards until I came to Reigate Heath where I struck over the heather and the soft mossy turf of the golf course towards the lofty black ruin of the windmill on the high knoll south-west.

There were isolated groups of tall pines swaying in the high north-east gale and all round me were young silver birch trees sparkling in the sun. A man was mowing one of the smooth greens of the golf course which runs in and out among the heather and the sandy combes.

I climbed up to the old mill which has a round brick base. It shares the summit of the knoll with a group of cottages. I am not surprised at the desire to live on this hill-top, for the view northward of the chalk-pits of the Downs is superb.

On the south-west side of the mill I went along a cinder track past the golf club-house and on joining the road left Dungate Manor and Heathfield on my left and followed it right-handed until it curved to the left. The road immediately on the right here has a notice "No thoroughfare," but the second turning to the right has a notice "Garthlands." I followed this which began by being a lane but soon bears to the right to become a carriage drive. But there is a sandy narrow bridle-path that goes on and that is the way I took. It soon changed its character to that of a very high-banked Devon hedged lane, and on the top of a rise I got the sweet smell of sawn wood and the man who was sawing assured me that I was on the right track for Leigh by way of the Mole.

I walked on contentedly. The way was well marked especially by horses' hoofs. There was certainly no sign of having to hew my way through undergrowth with a hatchet. It was just a little lost lane known well to horses and their riders and a few walkers. It led me down to join a wider lane going right where I passed a red house and then came to a derelict tall brick mill bearing the date 1740. Just opposite this mill I crossed a white narrow wooden bridge which led me over a field with a gun-emplacement in it overlooking the wide and deep Mole.

It is so seldom that any track in Surrey or Kent ever leads to a river bank that I now began to look forward to a

[Photo: Donovan E. H. Box
BETCHWORTH, VIEW OF CHALK-PITS

particularly pleasant walk alongside the Mole. Ahead I
could see several fields, each with its gun-emplacement and
the river winding very crazily in snake-like loops.

The path kept straight through several gates past a
remarkably fine oak tree in mid-field just above the river
and was green and well defined until I came to the red-
brick Ricebridge Farm where the woman of the house
came out to warn me that the soldiers had destroyed the
bridge over the river and that there was now no way

F

across. I did not want to leave the banks of the Mole so soon after reaching it, so I continued along a scarcely traceable track down to a gun-emplacement that was almost entirely hidden under a great bed of burrs. I fought my way through to the water's edge. It was a fearful struggle and I arrived at the edge with my coat and trousers covered with burrs, looking like a rugged Russian bear. There was no sign of a bridge. I could not battle my way back, so I went along the bank by a sort of jungle path made by previous walkers, probably the army, in single file, when they were building the pill-boxes. The river meandered tortuously below me. There was no way across except by swimming and it was far too cold for that. There was the semblance of a track along the edge of a ploughed field where I came to a gate. Here I read to my surprise this notice in red block capitals: "DANGER UNEXPLODED BOMB." There were two hedge-cutters nearby who amplified this warning. "Seven bombs fell altogether," they said. "It was in 1940—they located six—the seventh is in the bed of the river." They pointed to the place where I had fought my battle with the burrs. "They never found it. It's there for ever. The bridge has gone and they never repaired it." So the landmarks of England vanish. The gate bearing the forbidding notice gave on to the lane coming up from Ricebridge Farm and just on the right I came to a remarkably handsome red-brick farm with turkeys that showed great friendliness to me and began to follow me. The lane and the drive of this farm merged and led to the road at the top of the hill where I saw to my astonishment and amusement a notice pointing the way I had come by bomb and bridgeless river bearing these words—"Bridle-path and Footpath only." It was the only bridle-path notice that I had seen for weeks, and unless you took it to mean to Ricebridge Farm it led to the very dead end of the Mole's banks. There were three modern big brick houses of great splendour and charm on this rising ground, one with six gables, two-storeyed, long and low with superb views south over the weald and north to the nearby Downs. I felt that the people who live on this ridge must be uncommonly well off.

I turned right-handed at this bridle-path notice and was soon down at Flanchford Farm where the road from Reigate came in from the left. I turned right-handed and watched the Mole's slightly less wavering course as it came nearer to the bridge where I was now forced to cross it. This bridge is unexpectedly narrow and made of brick and the Army had placed concrete blocks and more pill-boxes to guard it. There was an attractive mill on the east side and altogether it was an admirable place to loiter and recover from the disappointment of the lost bridge. An elderly man and lady walking down the road stopped and asked me whether the bridle-path route was worth taking, On hearing my story they were certain it was and as a *quid pro quo* told me that .my best route was to leave the road and follow the west bank of the Mole past Bury's Court. "Once," said the man, "it was the family house of the Charringtons. Now it's an hotel in which we are staying." His instructions which were clear and precise lay

FLANCHFORD MILL POND

stress on our not missing the piggeries. They were the only thing I did miss. After the couple had gone on to search for our missing bridge and unexploded bomb I turned off the road by way of the concrete emplacements, took the quite clear green track that led along the banks of the Mole to a wooden bridge that carried me over one of the Mole's tributaries. The guest-house lay on rising ground straight ahead. It is of brick with decorative towers and a huge porch. I joined the drive that rather surprisingly made no effort to reach the front door but made a wide circuit round it above the Mole. Curiously enough I saw the only mole I have seen for months crossing this drive towards the Mole river. The drive made a wide circuit right round the house and became a lonely but clear gravelled cart-track which went straight for about half a mile and then turned sharp to the left.

It was here that I left it by turning right-handed over a gate to join an immensely wide green track with a water-wagon standing on it with a most neat contraption by which a quite young calf who had learnt how to work it got just the amount of pure water it needed by pushing its nose against a metal lever. The green way was so wide that it would have taken five or perhaps even six coaches abreast. I passed some pine woods on my right and a plantation with rides cut through on my left. There were several gates but always a clear track in the middle of the green way. It became narrower as I came to a gate with a farm on the left and an open upland field on the right. A strange very tall post suddenly appeared straight ahead to become my landmark. Had I kept on towards it I believe it would have led me right on to the road, but I turned away right through a gate along a track that almost at once petered out in an enormous pasture. When I reached the further side of this field I had some difficulty in finding the

[*Photo: H. D. Keilor*
THE OLD CHURCH, LEIGH

place to cross the stream, but the tiny shingled belfry tower spire of Leigh church suddenly appeared among the trees on the opposite slope and I was then able to recover the lost track over the stream. It was clear enough on the further side and brought me out as a field-path should, and nearly always does, exactly at the entrance to the church. The farmer had put a water-trough post and rails at the place where the stile should be.

The church is built of white Caen stone blocks, cut as the Romans cut their blocks for the Roman Wall. The carefully kept churchyard was full of rose bushes and inside I saw a large number of monuments to the Charringtons

[*Photo: Donovan E. H. Box*

"—A MOST FASCINATING MEETING OF FOUR CROSS ROADS WITH A
VILLAGE PUMP, A TETHERED SHEEP—"

and a notice announcing special Sunday half-hour services
for men. On the other side of the churchyard I came to the
Green, a fascinating meeting of four cross-roads with a
village pump, a tethered sheep, and a long low white
timber-and-plaster house of very great antiquity roofed
with Horsham stone and fenced in rather oddly. This is
known as the Priest's house, though it is no longer the
vicarage. The old school stands between the Charlwood
and Newdigate roads. Opposite I saw the general stores
and the white weather-boarded Plough inn where I got
one of the biggest surprises of my post-war wanderings.

The landlord was not only genial but only too ready to do what he could to provide a meal. "We'd have prepared a luncheon if you'd telephoned," he said. What he produced was new bread, fresh cheese, pickled onions, spam, home-grown tomatoes and as much beer as I wanted. A lorry man and a lean man with a curious bag who looked like a mole-catcher enjoyed the same fare. The conversation smacked of the real countryside. It ran on tree-felling. "He wields a good axe. He is a terrible good axer. He can swing an axe left and right," said the mole-catcher.

Wherever I went the greatest activity was the cutting, gathering, carting and storing of logs against the grim winter to come. There was talk of rabbits, of wages, and of the quality of the beer. "At Brockham I had a beer you could have cut with a knife." There was talking of cub-hunting, and I read the fixtures of the Surrey Union. Saturday. Park Gate, 8 a.m. Wed., Northlands Cross Roads, 7 a.m. Future dates included Newdigate Place, Rowhook and Chaffolds Farm Gate. I felt that if I were able to get out on all those dates I might discover even more of Surrey's lost footpaths. A tandem cyclist in shorts came in for a shandy, otherwise we had the place to ourselves. There were burnished brass cans round the shelves and many coloured electric lights over the bar. In the distance a canary carolled sweetly in the sun. It was a very memorable interlude. After my meal I went back to the church and while I was in it a farm labourer in corduroys came in, went up to the organ loft and began playing. He seemed like a character out of Thomas Hardy. "No! I'm not the organist," he said in answer to my query. "It's my dinner hour, and that's how I like spending it." I read the list of vicars; they go back to 1567.

It was nearly two o'clock before I took the way that led northward towards Betchworth, leaving the Plough on my right. I passed a house with fine ornamental iron gates on my right, a new village school and cottages on my left and then a Lilliputian thatched cottage called "Thatched Cottage." On the opposite side of the road that later went off to the right to Reigate I saw a nursery-man's announcement that he was prepared to sell cucumbers, spinach, tomatoes, onions and all sorts of desirable things, but his gate was locked. Further down on the right was the Seven Stars inn of Dawes Green, a weather-boarded inn of considerable size. An old man in the bar told me that the field-path to Brockham was easy to find, so on I went up the road, passing a fine house on the left with brick garden walls decorated by brick balls.

The cottages on the right-hand side of the road were quite enchanting, embowered among trees, with stone-flagged gardens, smooth lawns and orchards weighed down with apples. One was called "Sweet Briar."

I got a sense of a quiet, beauty-loving, unpretentious, happy community who probably spend their sunny Saturday afternoons in summer on the little green cricket field to watch the lads of the village uphold the honour of Dawes Green against all comers.

I saw a little yellow-haired girl come riding down the road and turn away down the road to Newdigate which went away on my left. It was just before I reached this road which is near two bus stops that I saw a well-defined stout stile and gate on the right giving me my direction. It faced due north and over the top of the field ahead I could see the chalk-pits of the North Downs. I kept along the right edge of the field, down to the next stile where there was a ditch spanned by a new little wooden bridge which surprised me. Then I turned half-felt over a stile where a bevy of goldfinches were chattering away among the thorns. The path now became completely obliterated over the next field, but as you can see the stile on the further side of the field it is easy to find the way. It was becoming increasingly evident to me that the only way to find your path across ploughed fields is by making a point to point from stile to stile.

I then came to a very clear cross-track which I crossed and kept on the left side of the hedge in front to the next gate and stile. There was now a wood on my left and the chalk-pits on the Downs were on my half-right. Then after the next stile came a short field which led to a bridge over a stream followed by a climb up the left side of a tall hedge. Here there was practically no trace of the track. I got over a gate on the left, leaving a farm with a tall poplar in front of it on my left, joined the farm track and was soon on the narrow road which ran east and west. I crossed this to join a green lane which ends sharply after a couple of hundred yards. At the top of this lane are three cottages and a gate with a track going off to the right. This which seems the obvious, indeed the only way, is wrong. There

[*Photo : H. D. Keilor*

is an exquisite secluded brick cottage with lawns and trees in the middle. On the left is a gate which bears a notice "Shut this Gate." It appears only to lead to a little garage, but just to the left of the garage and between the garage and another brick cottage on the left is our stile. It is quite difficult to see.

Once over the stile I found myself with the garden hedge of the lovely cottage on my right and then at the far end of the field is another stile.

For some odd reason the track then suddenly becomes clear again. It leads down the side of a wood, across a few fields, now appearing as a clear green and then as a worn track. I passed over a gate to a field of roots and then a second field of roots, the track not being obliterated in either field as it keeps close to the right-hand edge by the trees.

At the end I encountered a gipsy encampment of two caravans and five stalwart horses exactly where the track joins the road.

I crossed the road going right and left to take a wide margined lane going north with a succession of extraordinarily rich and tasteful mellow old brick houses with red-tiled roofs and tall brick chimneys. On the left was the Moat House Farm, with whitewashed walls, a white fence and a dry moat. Then came a succession of elms and then a remarkable red-brick house that seemed to be built round two colossal chimneys extending right to the ground; on the south side were four large dormer windows and a very steep red-tiled roof. On the north there was an equally imposing chimney but no windows at all. At the end of the lane I came to the white spired church of Brockham with a churchyard so beautifully trim that it would make a perfect bowling green. It overlooks the loveliest village green in England. It has earned immortality as the original of R. C. Sheriff's comedy "Badger's Green." The cricket ground is triangular and small. It is entirely surrounded by houses big and small of great variety and beauty. There are two trees on the northern side, a village hall, a brick house with blue painted windows and doors, a village store of great age and dignity and a suc-

[*Photo: Donovan E. H. Box*
BROCKHAM GREEN—THE OLD PUMP

cession of serene cottages that look like the cottages in "Cranford."

What makes this green so uncommonly lovely is the fact that behind it rise the steep curves of the green downs and the dazzling white of the chalk-pits. Indeed its setting is quite unforgettable.

Brockham may well stand for an epitome of the English village at its very best. There seemed no blot on its escutcheon, but the sexton told me that the children disliking tidiness do their best to undo his good work to keep the churchyard tidy. He didn't seem to mind. "That's just children's way," he said. Brockham breathes an air of affability and goodwill. At the top of the green when at last I could tear myself away I turned sharp left down Old School Lane and just after crossing the bridge over Tanner's Brook I turned right-handed past a red-brick house on to a rough wide track with a grass margin. As I walked the bells of Brockham church rang pleasantly in my ears. After passing over a ditch I saw the Betchworth golf course on my right and left, as rich and smooth a course as ever I saw, with broad smooth fairways and sandy bunkers and great trees rising up to a high wooded hill on my left. The track that curves its way right through the heart of the golf course reminded me of the Fosse Way in its straightness and loneliness. It climbed to a spot where I got a perfect view over the valley to the majesty of Box Hill and then the track swept quietly through a little copse to join a road as different as medieval England was from our modern world, the hustling bustling arterial road from Redhill to Dorking.

Luckily the water-mill is only a few hundred yards along after the junction of the roads and here I was able to get tea. It isn't always open.

I had had a rare adventure. The walk had occupied six hours and I had covered about fourteen enchanting miles of really rural and at times lost England.

A CORNER OF BETCHWORTH [*Photo: H. D. Keilor*

THE MOLE NEAR BOXHILL

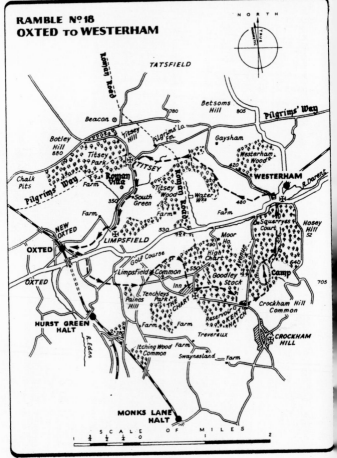

RAMBLE Nº 18
OXTED TO WESTERHAM

NORTH
TRUE
MAGNETIC

TATSFIELD

Roman Road

Beacon ⊙

Betsoms Hill 805

Pilgrims' Way

Botley Hill 880

Titsey Hill

Pilgrims' La.

Pilgrims' Fm.

Gaysham

Titsey Park

TITSEY

Westerham Wood

620

Chalk Pits

Pilgrims' Way

Roman Villa

Farm

South Green

350

Titsey Wood

Roman Road

Water Wks

480

WESTERHAM

R. Darent

Farm

Squerryes Court

Hosey Hill 52

NEW OXTED

LIMPSFIELD

Farm

530

Moor Ho.

590

High Chart

Avenue

640

Camp

705

OXTED

OXTED

Golf Course

Limpsfield Common

550

Inn

Goodley Stock

Tenchleys Park

Paines Hill

THE CHART

Farm

Farm

Reservoir

KENT HATCH

Crockham Hill Common

CROCKHAM HILL

HURST GREEN HALT

R. Eden

Trevereux

Itching Wood Common

Farm

Farm

Swaynesland

Farm

MONKS LANE HALT

SCALE OF MILES
1 ¾ ½ ¼ 0   1   2

Oxted, Limpsfield, Uvedale Road, Limps-
field Common, Golf Course, The Chart,
Kent Hatch, Crockham Hill Common,
Camp, Squerryes, Westerham, Titsey, Oxted

THIS turned out to be as variable and exciting a
walk as any I had undertaken.

On leaving Oxted station, I turned eastward and then
right-handed along Station road down the slope and half-
way up the further side where it joined a main road. I
crossed this and then took the first turning on the left up
Uvedale Road, which curves left-handed up the hill with
houses lying well back in wooded gardens.

A few hundred yards up I saw a revolving stile leading
into a twitten going steeply up between fences on my
left. I took this and within five or ten minutes I was on
the top of a wild sandy plateau of bracken, heather and
silver birches, a glorious waste land called West Heath.
There were houses facing the Heath on the left, so I turned
southward among the countless paths. There was an ugly
red-towered building that rose above the trees on my left
which turned out to be the Church Missionaries Children's
Home. I soon cut across Pollards Wood road and steered

LIMPSFIELD CHURCH

[*Photo: H. D. Keilor*

east along a sandy way down into a dip at the foot of which I found that I had a choice of no fewer than six ways.

By taking the broadest and greenest of these that led east over Limpsfield Common, I came to the meeting of four roads in the very heart of the heathland. There was a golf course on the further side eastward, so I followed this along the side of the fairway and at the far end found myself in a wood at Ballards Shrew overlooking a clearing to the north, so I turned southward into the wood again past a German prisoners-of-war camp which led me into Redlands Lane where I turned left past an oast-house at Redlands Farm. Here I took a footpath opposite the farm on the right past some new buildings and came out on Chart Common just by the Carpenter's Arms which has a wide wild open space in front of it. At the far end stands the squat spire of St. Andrew's on the Chart, a very clean and pleasant church built in 1896 with a white-washed wooden roof which makes it admirably light.

As a matter of fact there are scores of ways over Limpsfield Common which will bring you in the end to St. Andrew's church, but if you go further south than my route you may find your way complicated by having to thread your way among houses hidden on the heath.

Last time I did this walk, on leaving the church I turned into the woods on the south side of the road going eastwards. The criss-cross of tracks round Scearn Bank was so formidable that this time on leaving the church I turned north about a hundred yards to the north-eastern edge of the common where stands the Mill House to mark where the old windmill used to stand. Directly east of this house is a lamp-post standing exactly at the entrance into the vast woods of High Chart. I entered the woods here. The track was at first broad, a fine shady green way running among pines. Then came a choice of three ways. I chose the right and at the next fork bore left, crossed a prehistoric bank and shortly afterwards crossed what was obviously the vallum and fosse of the Roman road that cuts through these woods. There was little but rubble to be seen on the raised bank that ran along under thorns and gnarled ancient tree trunks.

Shortly after crossing the Roman road I turned up sharply to the right and then equally sharply to the left and then found my way narrowing to an overgrown bracken track with whortleberry bushes on either side. Then I came to the junction of four ways and I took the track that went south-east which brought me into the Long Walk, a magnificent broad ride going southward to the reservoir and northward to Westerham. This looks a most inviting path and if you wish to shorten this walk, turn left on this track and you will find that it takes you direct to Westerham. I turned right because I was in search of a view. Very soon the Long Walk brought me out in the road close by a great tree. Here I turned left and was soon at Kent Hatch, where I came to three very handsome ancient brick houses, the first on the right standing on the extreme edge of an escarpment as steep as any sea-cliff edge.

The view to the south was sudden and glorious, extending right over to Ashdown Forest and Crowborough. There is a seat at the junction of the roads at Kent Hatch where I sat in the sun and enjoyed the view while the spaniels from the big house came over to give me a friendly greeting.

According to the map there is a very inviting direct track running through Goodley Stock direct to Westerham. This is found by taking the road that turns north, not turning in by the track opposite the big brick house with the well in the garden, but by the wide track a little further on that runs at the back of two cottages.

I took the track that goes in opposite the big house and I think it is the better way. It begins, as so many of these tracks do, by being broad and easy to follow, and I liked it because it led me upwards on to Crockham Hill Common, a wild and lovely land of fine beeches, elms and pines and a galaxy of slim silver birch and ash trees. I saw a red cottage below in a deep gully of woodland. I came to the meeting of four tracks and veered to the north.

Then I suddenly got a clear view over the tree-tops to the woods of Sevenoaks. A great gully gaped on my right, so I veered left into an avenue of laurels and bracken. A fine group of tall birch trees on my left were succeeded by some curious wires laid across the track and then I came to a clearing covered with willow-herb. A derelict lorry stood in the track which abruptly changed its nature. The wood-cutters had been at work and stopped just here.

Five jays got up together and flew into a neighbouring group of oak trees. On my right I looked down from my hill-top into a big clearing of pasture land where cows were grazing. There was also a rather large cultivated clearing on my left. I was on the last spur of a once stupendous camp. By keeping left all the time I had a clear track and kept right on the crest of the ancient gigantic tree-covered knoll. It ended abruptly in a steep bracken track down which I slithered to find myself at a gate with green broad tracks coming in from the valleys on each side of the camp.

There was now a choice of three green ways, all of them cart-tracks, two going over and round the shoulder of a further hill, the third sweeping down and round the other rides of the park-like valley. I followed this track which brought me very soon to a succession of little lakes with fine oaks growing on the further hillside.

I had encountered no walkers all day, but now all Westerham seemed to be taking the sunny afternoon air in Squerryes Park. Children were paddling by the score in the streams that connected the lakes. This vast undulating wild park is indeed a tremendous boon to Westerham and obviously widely appreciated, for along the many tracks of the park I saw women collecting sticks for firewood, ladies airing their dogs, girls with baskets in search of hazel nuts, mushrooms and blackberries. There seemed to be no restrictions. It was a joy for once to see no barbed wire and no notices warning trespassers that they would be prosecuted. This is a perfectly kept vast park of great splendour, and I can think of very few places in England where so noble and huge a pleasance is free for everyone to roam.

The park ends in drive gates on the other side of which I came to a lake fringed with tall reeds. On my right over the water-meadows I saw a strikingly beautiful yellow-washed square house with tall rectangular windows. I followed the right-hand track past a singularly attractive terra-cotta brick cottage to a centuries-old worn stone stile past the allotments to a twitten. I crossed this at Bank Cottage to follow another twitten which I thought would

[*Photo : Donovan E. H. Box*
WOLFE'S STATUE, WESTERHAM

lead me to the church. I was surprised to find that it ended in the courtyard of the King's Arms, opposite the George and Dragon which bears a sign to the effect that General James Wolfe stayed there on his last visit to Westerham in December, 1758. The change from the deserted woods and quiet park to the over-crowded streets was startling.

I had tea at the Wolfe Café whence I looked out over a little green to a monument to the dapper little General Wolfe and beyond it to the vivid sign of the Grasshoppers inn. I then went across to have a look at the solid stone

TITSEY CHURCH

[Photo: Donovan E. H. Box

church which stands on a knoll. It was decorated for Harvest Festival. There were apples and marrows, tomatoes on the window-ledges and fruit and a few flowers on the pulpit, but no sheaves of corn and little sign of the old-time plenty. The villagers walked past the church door in great numbers, but nobody came in while I was there.

One of the most difficult things in these days of new roads and new housing estates is to find where any foot-path out of a town starts. Having reached Westerham I wanted to test whether the field-path to Titsey, so clearly marked on the map, was still as fictitious as it had been when I first tried to find it the other way. I asked several people and they all agreed that there was a footpath to Titsey but that it was rarely used. I had little difficulty in finding its starting-point. On leaving Westerham church I turned westwards, passed one turning to the right, and came to the second turning where was a signpost "Tatsfield 4 Croydon 12." I turned up this road past a fine brick house on the corner covered with creeper and turned in almost at once left-handed at a twitten marked with two white posts. This led straight up a paved way with new buildings on the right and old buildings on the left, past the allotments on to the common on the top where a football match was in progress (I was still to see a cricket match that same afternoon!). I crossed the ground diagonally to a road on the hill crest which I crossed to another road which kept along the top. I veered right almost at once and there saw the only signpost that I had seen indicating a footpath all day. It read "Footpath to Clacketts." I think that I shall return to this notice, take it down and present it to the British Museum. There is no such place as Clacketts on the map. There is no such place as Clacketts in existence.

I followed the alleged footpath along a narrow grass track with a garden hedge on my right which led me to a stile. On the other side of the next field I saw another stile on the edge of a wood. There was no track, but I made a point for the stile. From there I saw another stile at the edge of the next wood, so I crossed the next field diagonally with

THE BELL INN, OXTED

the wood on my left and landed safely at this stile. A well-defined track came in from the wood here and stopped abruptly. It must have been made by cattle. I then went through a gate and saw a very faint green track leading to the northern tip of another big wood on my left and again I made a point for the next stile. I kept going from right tip to right tip of the jutting-out woodland. The road was on my right and running almost parallel. The Downs were on my right and getting gradually nearer. There was a small farm on the roadside and in the field on my right a shooting party were banging away. But I got all the partridges, for I found that I was driving not less than a dozen brace in front of me in my pursuit of stiles.

I crossed a double post and rails over a ditch and found another stile in front and then a stile on the left of a field which was ploughed up. I was now veering west rather than north-west and had to cross a field of roots which ended in a road up which I turned right-handed for a few yards until I found a stile on the left-hand side and off I plunged again over two fields where I could see the stiles in gaps at the end of each field, but no connecting track. Then the stiles suddenly became very grand—two tall white and ornate pillars with wooden steps. I could see those easily from the further side of the fields. They were quite new and I can't imagine what their purpose can be. I didn't mind the absence of tracks. I still had my dozen brace of partridges as well as a few isolated cock pheasants for company. Then the stiles gave out altogether. I came to a fence which was wired with barbed wire on both sides. Luckily I could now see the spire of Titsey church, so I made a bee-line for that. I descended to a stream, spanned by an old brick bridge and by its side a stack of baled hay and then found myself in a narrow cinder lane up which I turned northwards and was soon at the top of the lane where I turned left for Titsey church. It took me exactly an hour from Westerham to Titsey and I had been making my way blind most of the way except for the intermittent stiles.

I suggest that the Ordnance Survey Department should revise their maps and either order these long untrodden paths to be brought into use again or delete meaningless tracks from their maps. I was on the Pilgrims' Way at Titsey. The lovely brick house opposite the church was obviously once a posting-house of importance and great charm. To-day Titsey is a dead end, for the park is private. It contains a Roman villa, but you aren't allowed to see it, and though the Pilgrims' Way cuts right through it, you aren't allowed to follow it.

[*Photo : H. D. Keilor*

VILLAGE CRICKET—"THE BAT GOES CRACK
AND LURES THE RAMBLER FROM THE TRACK"

For my part after my scramble over the lost land between Westerham and Titsey, I was grateful for the change of a road. It led me more or less straight south back to Limpsfield and Oxted where I spent the last remaining hours of daylight watching the leisurely last innings of the season of the Oxted cricketers who (believe it or not) were being entertained by a strident crooner on a loud speaker at a merry-go-round nearby which alternated between a Christmas carol in Latin and excerpts from "Annie, get your gun." Groups of German prisoners-of-war were watching the game with great interest. The scene was certainly peaceful and very English. The church bells were ringing and Oxted certainly boasts a very wonderful old church. The shadows were lengthening, the cricketers were in no hurry. They were 55 for 5 and as the other side had made 130 there was little prospect of a finish unless five wickets fell in half an hour.

It seemed difficult to believe that within a mile or two of this civilised comfortable cricket field there were woods so thick that you could be lost in them for hours and fields over which man no longer ever passed on his way to church or pub or work.

My day's walk was about 14 miles and in that space I had seen more than one palimpsest of an old community. It had been extraordinarily enjoyable but in its latest stages bristling with obstacles that should not be permitted to continue.

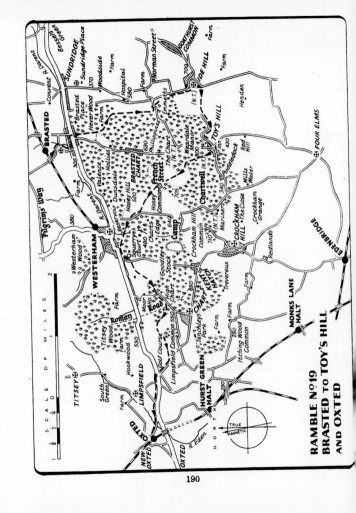

RAMBLE No.19
BRASTED to TOY'S HILL
AND OXTED

Brasted, Elliott's Lane, Hever Wood, Emmetts, Ide Hill, Toy's Hill, Weardale Manor, French Street, Hosey Common, Westerham, Squerryes Court, High Chart Limpsfield Common, Oxted

I BEGAN this walk from Brasted and I owe the enchanting first part to a little old woman who was washing her steps in the main street exactly opposite Elliott's Lane. The map gives no foretaste of the loveliness of the track that this little old lady shewed me.

"Indeed there is a straight footpath way to Ide Hill," she said, "and many's the time I've taken it. It starts just opposite between Mr. Webb's the chemist and Mr. Rice's the tobacconist's shop."

She pointed excitedly across the road. "And I only wish I could be coming with you," she said. "It's a grand lonely walk and there's beauty all the way." She was right. It was a clear enough track. There was an old notice high up on the left wall of the twitten testifying that it was a public footpath and a new notice on the right wall announcing that it was Elliott's Lane. It ran past some cottages, past an oast-house, then became narrower and led steeply up some steps between two upright posts. Then it ran between two fences, and later between a beech hedge on the right and a fence on the left. There was a view of fields on my right and some coarse grass and pine trees on my left. It became a little sandy lane and led to a small colony of cottages on my right. On my left was the undulating and pleasant park of Brasted Place, not so imposing as Westerham and obviously private. The cottages all bore a coat of arms which included a white sword. A lane came in from the right as I came to Hever Wood and I followed this down into a hollow and up again. A large flock of turkeys appeared in the field on my right where there was a farm with an oast-house. As I walked along the lane to the left I read a notice asking users to keep to the tracks. It seemed for once easy as there was only one track to keep to. It swept gracefully round the right edge of Hever Wood with what seemed a glacial valley winding in and out on my right filled now partly with sandpits and partly with fields of roots. A cart-track ran across my track to one of the sandpits, but I kept on my way which now became a leafy lane and was almost immediately crossed by another track.

I kept on straight ahead along a clear cart-track through a wood on an upland slope with a pleasant rounded gully of meadowland below on my right and on the other side of the gully grass slopes leading to more woods.

Three hunting spaniels and a golden retriever raced noiselessly across the valley in front of me, failed to notice me and went on with their work, disappearing into the woods on my right. I came down to the gate that they had come through and climbed up the other side.

The woods closed in a little and the lane became a less noticeable track on the left edge of the field. I heard the distant church bells of Brasted ringing for Harvest Thanksgiving. I came over a rise and down to another gate where the track became much greener with ploughland on my left. It was now a fenced way going up the centre of a gully with a wood on my right. Straight ahead five enormous turkeys occupied the whole of the top of the gate and stile that I had to pass through. Very neatly hidden away on the right between two shoulders of a hill stood the farm of Quornden. The turkeys were so certain that I had come to feed them that they followed me through the gate up to the stile at the top of the field where I met the road leaving the farm well on my right.

As soon as I got to the road I turned left but almost at once came to a stile on the right which led me straight across the drive leading to Emmetts and as soon as I got to the gate on the further side I got a superb view of the tall thin spire of Ide Hill church perched on the top of the knoll on my half-right. I had expected to find it far more to the left.

I went through the gate and found a track over an open field from which I got a grand view not only of the coy village of Ide ahead but of the whole wooded hillside of Sevenoaks away to the east. The field-path led me to a kissing-gate on the roadside where I turned right with the

[Photo: H. D. Keilor

ENJOYING THE VIEW FROM IDE HILL

huge square house of Emmetts standing grandly on the summit of the hill on my right. Two girls on grey ponies were trotting down the drive to the Ide road. Very soon I was in the centre of the upland village. Outside the Crown was a third girl on a grey pony. I crossed the unkempt village green which has two jolly weather-boarded cottages on the southern side, and entered the drive just below the church which leads to the wonderful viewpoint on the extreme southern edge of the escarpment that belongs to the National Trust. This is a sort of nose or promontory of smooth grass with seats among the bracken, broom, gorse and silver birches. The view extends over Penshurst, Hever, Chiddingstone and Edenbridge just below to the whole range of the Ashdown Forest in the distance.

Westward just over a deep green gully I saw the many rich and rare red-roofed houses of Toy's Hill clustering cosily among the woods. I should say that Ide Hill was far more exposed. I sat for some time on Ide Hill in complete solitude enjoying the rare treat of this stupendous view. Then I went back along the unkempt green, past the village pump and exactly opposite the Crown inn I turned westwards past a fine red-brick house the windows of which commanded a view of the whole weald below. The way here is so well trodden that I began to visualise a constant intercommunication between the walkers of these two villages, perhaps to compare their views at different seasons of the year. Anyway here for once I was on a track that was used. It was to my surprise being used on this occasion by three cyclists whom I met carrying their bicycles up the very steep green fields that I was sliding down. They were probably doing it for a bet. They didn't appear to be liking it much. As I looked back at the path I saw the tip of the spire of Ide Hill church peeping coyly above the brow of the hill as if beckoning the cyclists on, but they were now in midfield resting. At the foot of the hollow I came to a wooden bridge over a stream and then followed a choice of two ways. I took the left fork because it was a wider track, a rutted cart-track which led me to a gate and a stile and then walked along the right-hand edge of an open field on the slopes with a fine view of the weald below and of Ide church on the hill on the other side of the valley. The track swept round this field and revealed a far larger number of lovely warm and ancient red-tiled and red-brick houses on the hillside than I had expected to see.

Not, I felt, an ideal place to live during a petrol shortage, but perfect for those who only want a house with a view.

I passed over a stubble field full of hens, to another with two grey ponies in it and then came to a group of farm buildings nestling on the hillside. The way on lies to the left of the new farm but to the right of the older lovelier red-roofed house which has an open-air bathing pool standing just in front of some yew trees. Another comfortable-looking red-brick house with trim gardens stood above the track which to my intense surprise was here marked by a completely new stile. I hadn't seen a new stile in a hundred miles of walking. The track here led very steeply up the wooded hillside to turn left-handed into a lane which was lined with a whole succession of extremely beautiful houses. England, I felt, could not be in such desperate financial straits with so many scores of these obviously expensive houses every mile or so. What struck me as odd was the fact that every house was in such an excellent state of repair with new fences, new roofing and new out-buildings.

The first house in this lane has a magnificent thatched roof. The next house where the gardeners were carrying apples in great baskets into the house had lovely latticed windows and a circular covered well in the middle of the lawn.

I passed a concreted oast-house, then a big house in the hollow with a vast circular stone terrace in front of the house like a giant turntable for cars to turn easily.

Then I came to Tally Ho! cottages and the Tally Ho! inn at the four cross-roads. As on my last visit there was no attempt on the part of the drinkers in the bar to emit hunting noises as I entered. They all looked lugubrious and spoke in undertones. There was a photograph on the wall of a shooting party but as most of the men were wearing Dundreary whiskers I felt that few of those photographed were likely to be present in the bar. Just outside the inn there stands a signpost indicating that the westward road leads to Puddledock.

A few yards along this road I came to the terrace with its well, wall and walk that were presented to the nation by the late Mr. Frederick Feeney of Beckhampton. The wall was given by Octavia Hill to the village in 1898. The view from here is supposed to extend over seven counties on a clear day. This is one of the earliest of all National Trust gifts and attracts a great number of visitors who are completely in the dark about the meaning and purpose of this beneficent organisation. The ground below the wall falls away as steeply as the street of Clovelly and like Clovelly has little picturesque cottages clinging to its sides like limpets. On leaving the walk I retraced my steps nearly to the signpost, then turned up left-handed past the National Trust notice through an opening on to a high small common in a clearing of the woods. High above the common, almost hidden among the bracken, I found the Ordnance Survey viewfinder which gave the directions and distances of about thirty prominent landmarks. I was surprised to read that St. Paul's Cathedral was only 20 miles away as the crow flies. Indicators pointed to Rye (34), Portsmouth (59), Windsor (35), Canterbury (42), Eastbourne (34) and Dover (53) miles away. None of these places was visible to the naked eye that day, but there was a yellow light under the whole ridge of Ashdown Forest that gave that noble line a queer radiance.

On leaving the Ordnance mark I turned north-west, and after twisting and turning along the narrow and tortuous tracks through the bracken I came to a well-marked path running parallel with and close to a fence on its left. I followed this up a very steep bank to the ending of the fence, then passed a plantation of thick small trees as I went downhill with only bits of old fencing on the right. I descended an oak wood very steeply, crossed a cross-track where the left of the track was full of gnarled old oaks, saw a pine drive going off on to the right, but the way was partially barred by a tree trunk laid across the path. I kept left-handed on the path which descended further and further into the depths where I passed a tall blue pine and saw a sad old deserted walled garden and weeds growing from twelve to fifteen feet high. This was all that is left of Weardale Manor. A track runs back southward here to Chartwell, the home of Mr. Winston Churchill, but the way to it is private and my way lay northward, a wide sandy clean track running between fences across a gully where another track comes down the hill from the right to join it. I saw three oast-houses on the eastern slopes of the ravine, then I passed through a gate to a gravelled drive to French Street, where there is a fine remodelled farm with two oast-houses with white sword-like poles jutting out from their cowls, and a very up-to-date set of entirely new outbuildings. There were scores of tons of coal and massive piles of wood ready for the winter, so I imagine this farm must be run on a lavish scale. This house stands secluded in a dell exquisite in its form, quiet, dignified and very warm-looking by virtue of its old red tiles on roof and walls.

A new road has been made entirely for the sake of this house, and new stiles where the path curves steeply round the hill to the hamlet of French Street, which is a colony of small houses of great antiquity that have been modernised. The most charming is April Cottage which is built of black timbers and white plaster, has latticed windows, red-tiled roof and wonderfully kept lawns. It looks out across the quiet smooth gully eastward. Just beyond April Cottage is a stile leading on to a slope where families were picnicking above a new plantation of larch. I sat on this stile in the afternoon silence for some time admiring the enchantment of April Cottage and the quiet fields below. Then I continued on my way up the street of the hamlet and was not surprised to find that a plot of this ground had been acquired by George Barry of St. James' Street for his private burial ground.

The track led me on to Hosey Common where I was once more in a wild land of birch and beech and oak and ash with tracks going off left and right, but I kept on the newly-made road until I came out on the common on Hosey Hill where the track joined the main road. I turned right, and almost at once found a passage leading off to the left which brought me past the garden hedge of a little red house of tiles and lattice windows and smooth lawns and so over a stile into the great park overlooking Westerham. The track straight ahead led me past the reservoir down to cross a stone bridge over the water and I came out on to the Oxted road at the west end of Westerham village exactly at the Antique Tea Rooms where I had an excellent tea in a room decorated with Honour Boards of the Shooting VIII of Westerham School.

After tea I went along the road westwards, stopping to find some fresh architectural joy at every turn. The Tudor House I admired for its stone terraces, Pitt's Cottage for its lattice windows, the house opposite for its oval iron

[Photo: Donovan E. H. Box

PITT'S COTTAGES, WESTERHAM

201

CHART CHURCH

[Photo: H. D. Keilor

gateway. Each Westerham house is of old red brick, but each Westerham house has its own strong individuality. It must contain more rich and handsome houses to the square mile than any other village in England.

I turned left down the Edenbridge road past the big square brick mansion of Squerryes Court which has a large lake in front of it, and I turned in right exactly opposite the farm buildings and took the stile just on the left of Orchard House and a steep-pitched barn which has the text "Be Sober, Be Vigilant, 1868" painted on it. On my right I saw

BRASTED CHURCH

[*Photo : H. D. Keilor*

the huge walled garden of yet another imposing many-windowed brick house. I found the field-track to be quite clear. It runs on the left side of a hedge with the stile in the wood on the slopes above visible all the way. Inside the wood I found the shady track going off just a little to the left, but still quite unmistakable. Here I caught up with a man who was carrying a very sizeable log by a rope back to his car. The fuel shortage has turned us all into forest looters. The woods in the High Chart are thick and there was a profusion of bracken and whortleberry bushes under the trees that made the going off the main path very

OXTED CHURCH

[Photo: H. D. Keilor

difficult. But the track led directly to the road where I turned left-handed inside the wood but parallel with the road which was quite quiet and ran through the heart of the forest. Soon I came to a junction of roads. The left goes to Chart Church, the right to Redland. I followed the right road till it came out to an open common with a smoothly rolled cricket ground on my left and the tower of Chart Church clearly visible beyond the green. I turned right-handed here down a cinder track which led me to the woods and skirted left-handed round a large field on my left. It was quite easy to follow. It kept in the wood all the way, a deep cutting round a field of roots. I could see fields through the trees on my right. I came to a sandy cross-track which I crossed to the opposite wood which was full of mountain-ash trees and conifers. I emerged on to a green space with a stile opposite leading to a green track with a raspberry plantation on my left. This led me into more woods at the end of which I came out on to the edge of the Limpsfield golf course where I walked straight ahead over the fairway and across three or four intersecting cross-roads until I came to the red tower of the Children's Home. Here I threaded my way across the mazy ways of West Heath and so down the twitten to Uvedale road, across the main Godstone road half-right, and so down to the station at Oxted.

This walk took me seven hours and was about fifteen miles. When I got back to Oxted village I found that in spite of the fading light the cricketers were still playing. I left them to it in order to go off to visit again the old church which has nothing quite so interesting as its very short and dominating tower but does contain a number of brasses, a monument to a Tudor knight whose 17 children are all represented, and some typical Victorian stained glass windows.

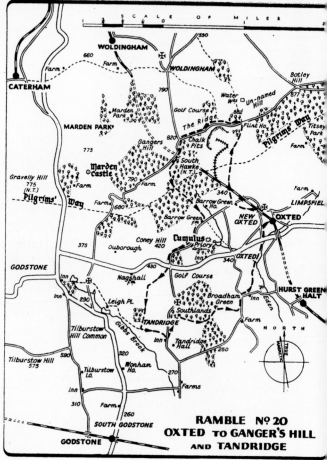

RAMBLE No 20
OXTED TO GANGER'S HILL
AND TANDRIDGE

Oxted, Chalk Pit Lane, Downs, the Ridge, Gangers Hill, South Hawke, Barrow Green, Priory, Gibbs Brook, Barley Mow, Tandridge, Southlands, Broadham Green, Oxted Mill, Oxted.

I FOUND this to be a walk of extraordinary variety, combining steep downland climbing with gentle meadowland, wild woods with open fields and magnificent views of a most unexpected kind in most unexpected directions.

I first made my way north of Oxted station to the track that runs westward past the south door of the church. This led me to a track going half-right and then left over a big field facing the tremendous chalk-pit. At the end of the field looking back I got a fine view of the old stone church tower at the far end. This track brought me out in a lane where I turned left and then almost immediately bore right up Chalk Pit lane which ran under the railway bridge and then steeply up the hill.

It is a hedgeless lane, and I left it almost at once to climb on to the smooth downland on my right just by a couple of haystacks. You can see the chalk track in front going straight up, and long before you reach the summit you will feel that you have ascended well over the 882 feet that the Ordnance map declares the summit to be.

The point is that it is labour well rewarded, for the view from the crest of the downs is finer by far than the vista from Ide or Toy's Hill, and looks out over the greater part of the weald of Surrey and Sussex. You realise then for the first time how dense are the woods on Limpsfield Common and High Chart and how very well-wooded is the land between Oxted and Godstone.

Although this particular viewpoint has no name I think you will agree that the view is at least as fine as, and even more extensive than, that from the more famous viewpoint of Colley Hill. It is certainly a stiff sharp climb and you will have earned both the view and the rest by the time you get to the top.

There is a wood right on the top through which the track runs north to rejoin the lane near a house on the right called Whistler's Steep.

The big house in front with red-brick walls adjoining the walled-in garden is called Flint House. It stands at the north-west corner of four cross-roads, the north being a bridle-path to Warlingham. I turned westward along the way marked Woldingham, leaving the handsome square gazebo in the south wall of Flint House on my right. This western way runs along the crest on the extreme edge of the top of the chalk-pit which is here as intimidating as any sea cliff. The view is superb and gets better and better as

ON GANGER'S HILL, NEAR OXTED

the country to the south lies quite open. On the north there is a trim brake of tall fir trees.

I met a man coming out from the northern fields with a basket full of mushrooms, otherwise I met no one on the hill-top. Then came a succession of very handsome houses standing back among trees on both sides of the way which is here called the Ridge.

I passed a pillar-box at Wood Rising and at Foxbury, which has a fine timbered arched gateway. Workmen were rebuilding the brick and timbered stables. One south-facing garden had an ornamental iron gateway and a long grassy avenue that provided a wonderful view of all the land far down in the valley below.

The Ridge ends at a meeting of three ways where there is a signpost west of the North Down road, which leads to Woldingham. The land falls away providing a new and totally unexpected view north-west over the rolling country north of Redhill. My way lay south-west through a succession of lovely woods on Gangers Hill. These woods which boast some exceptionally tall and beautiful beech trees are known as South Hawke and belong to the National Trust. There are paths going through them in all directions and there is one specially inviting track on the left delving deep down the southern slopes that you may feel inclined to take.

Avoid doing so and keep along the ridge or in the wood parallel with it until the road turns slightly to the right. Here the track goes straight on in a line with the road behind. It is carpeted with beech leaves and very well-defined, and descends gently and diagonally south-westward along the densely wooded slopes of the downs.

This is obviously a very ancient way, probably one of the many tracks of the Pilgrims' Way. It is lined not only with very ancient beeches whose smooths trunk bear generations of initials, but also with yew trees whose thick girths betoken an incredible age. This is a very witchy wood which conjures up visions of masked highwaymen lurking in the shadows.

It is certainly a wood with a very strongly individual atmosphere. It veers due south as it gets to the lower slopes and when it reaches a clearing it crosses a track going east and west that is clearly defined on the east but seems to fade out in the west. I carried on due south down the woodland track. The fields on my right and left provided me with a good view of the downs each way. A man on my distant left disappeared into the lower woods with a gun. The woods closed in again and the track wound its clear way on under the beech trees until it became a quiet farm lane and came out at the foot of the hill with the lodge and huge red-brick house of Barrow Green House on my immediate left. I bore right alongside and above a brook up a slope to the very attractive three-storeyed timber and brick farm of Barrow Green on my right. On each side of the lane was a notice "Bridle-path only."

On the opposite side of the road where the track comes out is an iron footpath gate leading over the fields back to Oxted. I did not take this but turned right-handed along the quiet lane past the fine Priory on my left with a well-wooded park and a lake over which a solitary heron was flying. There is a tumulus close by but I couldn't see it. I climbed past the sandpit on Coney Hill and in the dense woods of the park on my left saw the huts of a big military camp.

This is close to the junction of four cross-roads and immediately opposite the lane from which I emerged stands a stile. The track straight on south-west to Leigh Place is clearly defined on the map, but on climbing over the stile I saw nothing but an unbroken ploughed field. I had no alternative but to skirt the field left-handed until I came to the opening in the fence where the second stile had once stood. Again there was no track across, but it was stubble land and I could see the stile on the further side. There is a long avenue crossing the track to this second stile. I forged straight over the stubble field leaving farm buildings in the hollow on my left and a lodge gate at the far end of the avenue on my right. The third stile led me into a lane and there was no sign of a stile on the other side of the lane, but about ten yards to the left I found a gate and a very clearly defined cart-track going round the top of an upland field above a gully. This is an excellent viewpoint. Looking back northward I got a grand view of the ridge of the North Downs from which I had come, as far west as Marden's Folly.

Southward the land fell gracefully and gently away to the wooded weald. I turned right-handed along the sandy cart-track which led me past a large tarred barn on my right and then past some very curious ivy-covered ruins. As the

[Photo: H. D. Keilor
THE BARLEY MOW INN, TANDRIDGE

walls were round and very thick I suspected the remains of an old castle, but the map made no mention of a castle, so it may have been an oast-house. Over to my right I saw the spire of Godstone church and from a gate on my right a little further on I looked over to the sandpits and high woods of Tilburstow Hill. The track led down a slope, and just about halfway down the hill a well-trodden path came in from Leigh Place and I turned along this sharp left just above Gibbs Brook. This led down the field and then up through a thick tall plantation, over a stile on to a sandy track with a field of roots on my right. Very soon I was out

OLD MILL, OXTED   *[Photo: Donovan E. H. Box*

in the lane with the notice "St. Denis Orchard" facing me and council houses standing above me on my left. I turned right and across the road entered the Barley Mow, Tandridge, where there was no food, but plenty of talk about dogs and some beer. The way on lies at the back of the Barley Mow where there is a lane.

You have to watch your way very carefully here, because the lane immediately becomes a footpath going up to the left. There is, however, a small cottage with a tall chimney on the right of this obvious track and on the right of this cottage there is a very tiny path unobtrusively stealing away up through a narrow gap. This is the way.

This is the beginning of an enchanting walk of which you would never guess the existence unless you had been forewarned. I came out of the narrow gap into a twitten and climbed over a rising field, saw in front of me an enormous walled garden with a great tower behind it. There were two ways around the walled garden, right and left. There were two gardeners working in the vast garden. By dint of shouting I attracted their attention but the walls were so high and I was so hidden by trees that they couldn't see me. I discovered that the gardens were those of Southlands and that my way lay right-handed along the south wall. This way was narrow and lay between a wall and fence. It took me under an ancient wooden footbridge connecting the house and the woods and then became a gentle bridle-path running along a ridge of woodland.

This track went on so long that I thought I had miscalculated my way. Then I saw an enormous square grey stone mansion in a hollow on my right and my way became a track through a fir plantation which brought me out to the edge of the woods to a house on my left with white gates. I then descended down to a group of attractive cottages to a rather untidy looking green with the main road running north and south through it and one road with a signpost on my half left going eastward.

I crossed the green, took this road which has a signpost which read Limpsfield and about a hundred yards on the right came to the Haycutter inn. Exactly opposite this inn is a curious little stile leading over a field northward. I

WINTER BEAUTY—THE OLD MILL POND, WESTERHAM

crossed a cross-track at the end of the field and the track
then led me across a field of roots with a stream running
on my right.

Then came a very green field which led me to the tall
red-brick derelict mill of Oxted. Turning right-handed,
leaving the pond on my left and the mill on my right I
turned in left-handed to another field and soon found
myself on the bank of the very clear and narrow mill-
stream which was blue with forget-me-nots. This bank-
path brought me to a stile that led me to a narrow stone

216

bridge and then up to a twitten between a house and a white cottage. This led to a deep cutting of a road where I bore left with the great roots of trees above me. Then ahead I saw the railway high above on an embankment and turned up a very narrow twitten half left that ran steeply up between the fences of gardens and then above another very deep cutting of a lane. At the top I came to the East Hill House Hotel and looked down on the village green of Oxted.

I had been out about 4½ hours and covered in all about nine miles of exquisite downland and meadow by-paths whose quiet loveliness could never be guessed from the map or the road.

My general feeling at the end of these twenty rambles is that Southern England still contains infinite wealth and infinite variety. The number of extremely handsome houses drives me to the conclusion that we are still individually wealthier than we imagine, and the infinite variety of lovely walks proves that in spite of depredation and obstacles we are unlikely in our time to exhaust the charms of our countryside. The going, in other words, is still good.

INDEX

CHEAP FARES FOR PARTIES OF EIGHT OR MORE

PARTIES of Adults, numbering eight or more, can travel at single fare for the double journey if going on a day or half-day's outing. For Athletes, too—cricket, football, hockey, etc., players and the officials of their clubs—there are reduced day fares, providing that the party numbers eight or more. There are also reduced rates for Children's Parties (minimum eight children) on day outings, and it should be noted that the half-price age for them *is extended to 16 years.*

In addition, for all **large parties** there are extra concessions.

For further particulars enquire of Local Stationmaster, or write to the Commercial Superintendent, British Railways, Southern Region, Waterloo Station, S.E.1

CONVENIENT CHEAP

[These fares are liable to revision]

To the principal places

†"Go as you Please" Cheap Day		TO	‡"Monthly Return"		Best L'don Dep. Sta.	Other London Dep. Stations (Note. — Fares from these stations may vary slightly)
1st	3rd		1st	3rd		
8/11	5/5	Betchworth............	11/-	7/4	Vic.	A, B, C, D, F
—	4/6	Boxhill and Burford Bridge (for Mickleham)	—	6/1	W'loo	A, B, C, D, E, G, H
—	5/-	Brasted	—	7/-	Ch.X	B, C, D, E, G, H
—	4/11	Dorking North	—	6/6	W'loo	A, B, C, D, E, G, H
—	—	Farnham	15/11	10/7	,,	—
—	—	Godalming	14/9	9/10	,,	—
—	—	Gomshall and Shere (via Dorking North and Deepdene)......	—	8/2	,,	D, E
10/7	6/1	Guildford	12/3	8/2	,,	D, E, G, H
	6/4					
—	—	Haslemere (for Hindhead)	17/8	11/9	,,	—

Children 3 and under 14 years, half fare.

Key to London Stations : A—Charing Cross ; **B**—Waterloo (via London Bridge); **C**—Cannon Street; **D**—London Bridge; **E**—Victoria; **F**—Waterloo (via Clapham Junction); **G**—Blackfriars; **H**—Holborn Viaduct.

†**"Go as you Please"** Cheap Day Tickets. For days of issue enquire at stations. These tickets are valid for return by any train same day from various stations at will (subject to excess fares being paid where necessary).

‡**"Monthly Return"** Tickets. These tickets are issued between any two stations on ANY DAY by ANY TRAIN (except "Liner" and "Continental" Boat Trains), available forward or return any day within one month (for one return journey) with break of journey at any intermediate station.

Note: The fares shown are those ruling on and from 1st March, 1948

FARES FROM LONDON
mentioned in this book
[These fares are liable to revision]

†"Go as you Please" Cheap Day		TO	‡"Monthly Return"		Best L'don Dep. Sta.	Other London Dep. Stations (Note. — Fares from these stations may vary slightly)
1st	3rd		1st	3rd		
—	6/4	Holmwood (for Leith Hill)	—	8/2	W'loo	A, B, C, D, E, G, H
		Horsham—				
—	—	via Worcester Pk...	—	9/10	,,	
—	—	via Sutton or Three Bridges	15/11	10/7	Vic.	D
—	—	Milford	14/9	9/10	W'loo	—
—	—	Ockley (for Capel)...	—	8/6	,,	D, E
7/4	4/5	Oxted (for Limpsfield)	9/2	6/1	Vic.	A, B, C, D, F
8/-	4/9	Reigate	9/9	6/6	,,	A, B, C, D, F
		Rudgwick—				
—	—	via Guildford	17/8	11/9	W'loo	D
—	—	via Horsham..........	17/-	11/4	Vic.	D, E
—	—	Warnham	—	9/10	W'loo	D, E
—	5/2	Westerham.,.........	—	7/-	Ch.X	B, C, D, E, G, H
8/8	5/2	Woking (for Chobham)	10/6	7/-	W'loo	E, G, H

Children 3 and under 14 years, half fare.

Key to London Stations : A—Charing Cross ; B—Waterloo (via London Bridge); C—Cannon Street; D—London Bridge; E—Victoria; F—Waterloo (via Clapham Junction); G—Blackfriars; H—Holborn Viaduct.

†**"Go as you Please"** Cheap Day Tickets. For days of issue enquire at stations. These tickets are valid for return by any train same day from various stations at will (subject to excess fares being paid where necessary).

‡**"Monthly Return"** Tickets. These tickets are issued between any two stations on ANY DAY by ANY TRAIN (except "Liner" and "Continental" Boat Trains), available forward or return any day within one month (for one return journey), with break of journey at any intermediate station.

Note: The fares shown are those ruling on and from 1st March, 1948

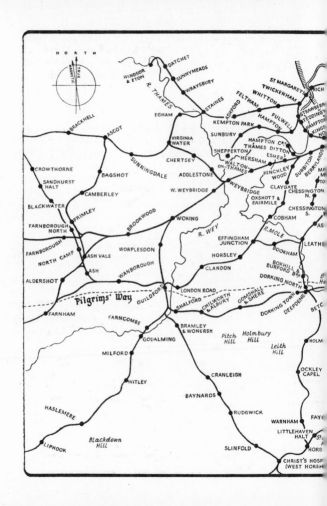